Dictionary of Environmental Terms

R

DICTIONARY
OF
ENVIRONMENTAL
TERMS

Alan Gilpin

Routledge & Kegan Paul
London and Henley

First published in Great Britain in 1976
by Routledge & Kegan Paul Ltd
39 Store Street,
London WC1E 7DD and
Broadway House,
Newtown Road,
Henley-on-Thames,
Oxon RG9 1EN
Printed in Great Britain by offset lithography by
Billing & Sons Ltd, Guildford, London and Worcester

ISBN 0 7100 8483 8

Preface

Few words in the English language are quite so all-embracing as the word "environment", a word indicating everything external to an organism, which itself is part of the environment of other creatures.

Restraint must prevail, therefore, particularly in a Dictionary such as this of modest proportions; the terms included have been selected in a somewhat pragmatic manner, partly on the basis of those most frequently encountered by the writer within the context of environment protection responsibilities largely concerned with pollution in all its forms and its control, and partly on the basis of the kind of terminology heard at, and embodied in the supporting documents of, the first United Nations Conference on the Human Environment held in Stockholm in 1972.

Comments by users which might be useful in considering later revisions of, and additions to, this Dictionary will be welcomed and appreciated.

The assistance of those who have courteously given permission for the reproduction of diagrams and photographs is gratefully acknowledged.

A. G.
Melbourne
Victoria
September, 1974

List of Illustrations

Figures

1. Rye Meads Sewage Works, England   3
2. Submersible device (known as a Store Unit) for measuring and recording dissolved oxygen and temperature in rivers and other bodies of water   42
3. Fumigation   62
4. City Bores, Rotorua, New Zealand   65
5. The hydrological cycle   76
6. Temperature inversion   80
7. Katabatic wind   81
8. A mobile lidar system used by the Central Electricity Research Laboratories in England for research into the dispersion of chimney plumes   87
9. Vicoma System for the containment of oil spills at sea   114
10. Craft-mounted device for reclaiming oil from a harbour or inland water-way   115
11. Oxygen sag curves relating dissolved oxygen content against time of flow   117
12. Map of the windscale area showing controus of radio-iodine contamination in milk on 13 October 1957   132
13. High Marnham Power Station, near Neward, Nottinghamshire, England.   162

Tables

1. Air pollutants with recognized or potential long-term effects on health at usual air-pollution levels   5
2. Geological time scale   64
3. Selected water pollutants having potential long term effects   172

List of Abbreviations

g	gram
g/m^3	grams per cubic metre
kg	kilogram
kg/h	kilograms per hour
km	kilometre
m	metre
m^2	square metre
m/s	metres per second
mg	milligram
$mg/m^2/d$	milligrams per square metre per day
N/m^2	newtons per square metre
μg	microgram
$\mu g/m^3$	micrograms per cubic metre
μm	micron or micrometre
mg/l	milligrams per litre
$\mu g/l$	micrograms per litre
ng/l	nanograms per litre
ppm	parts per million (in air pollution measurements, parts per million by volume; in water pollution measurements, parts per million by weight)
MW	megawatt

In water quality 1 ppm = 1 mg/l = 1 g/m^3

A

Abiotic   Non-biological; thus an abiotic element is a physical or chemical feature of an ecosystem *q.v.*, or environment. *q.v.*
   See Biotic.

Abyssal Zone   The cold, dark, water zone of the ocean depths, below the euphotic zone *q.v.*; it corresponds roughly to the profundal zone *q.v.* of the lake habitat. No photosynthesis *q.v.* can occur at this level and animal life is sparse.

Acclimatization   The process of phenotypic *q.v.* variation, as distinct from genetic variation, during which an organism undergoes morphological and/or physiological adaptation in response to various abiotic *q.v.* elements in the ecosystem *q.v.*, e.g. a response to nutritional levels or different altitudes or climates.

Accommodation   The location of a population *q.v.* within a specific geographical area or volume of habitat *q.v.*

Acid Soot   or acid smut. An agglomeration of carbon particles held together by moisture which has become acidic through combination with sulphur trioxide; soot particles range in size from about 1 mm to about 3 mm in diameter. The carbon particles are mainly coke spheres produced during combustion. Acid soot emitted from chimneys, leaves brown stains on materials and damages paintwork; the brown stain is caused by iron sulphate. The problem has been mainly associated with oil-fired installations equipped with metal chimneys. The potential hazard can be reduced by using fuels of relatively low sulphur content; operating plant with a minimum of excess air in order to reduce the formation of sulphur trioxide; elimination of air in-leakage to flues; the raising of back-end temperatures; the use of additives; the insulation of chimneys and ductwork; or by a combination of such measures.

Acoustic Reflex   The mechanism by which the ear protects itself from extra loud sounds by in fact reducing them; just as the eye protects itself from extra bright light by contracting the pupil. When sound enters the ear, the waves pass through the ear-canal to the eardrum which vibrates. The eardrum conducts these vibrations to three tiny bones or "ossicles". The ossicles change the loudness of sound before it enters the inner ear. The ossicles normally amplify soft sounds and dampen loud sounds as the connecting muscles contract or relax in response to the pressure of the sound waves. However, this mechanism operates successfully only over a certain range and its response is too slow to protect the ear from a sudden noise, e.g. a gunshot. Pain occurs as the ear unsuccessfully attempts to protect itself.

See also Sound Wave.

Acre-foot   The volume of liquid or solid required to cover one acre to a depth of one foot.

Activated Sludge Process   An aerobic *q.v.* process utilized in the secondary treatment *q.v.* plants for sewage; organic wastes are brought into contact with biologically active micro-organisms (in returned sludge) in the presence of mechanically introduced air. The activated sludge process is in effect an artificially accelerated self-purification process. When untreated sewage is mixed with a sufficient amount of biologically active sludge a rapid clarification takes place, the finely divided suspended and dissolved solids in the sewage being transferred to the surface of the sludge floc in which large numbers of organisms are concentrated. An artificial supply of air enables the organisms to continue their work of purification. A continuous supply of active sludge is mixed with the incoming sewage, and this necessitates returning a portion of the sludge obtained from the final settling tank to the sewage before it enters the activated sludge tank. The most common method of introducing oxygen into the sewage is to blow compressed air through porous plates placed in the bottoms of the tanks. Under-water paddles assist in the distribution of the air and help to keep the sludge in suspension. Improved designs of brush or blade-type surface aerators and other devices have increased the efficiency with which air is introduced into the aeration tanks. The sewage after passing through the activated sludge tanks is allowed to settle in secondary sedimentation tanks. After a detention time of two hours, the

activated sludge (other than that mixed with fresh sewage) is pumped to sludge digestion chambers
See Secondary Treatment. *Also* Figure 1.

Figure 1   Rye Meads Sewage Works, England, showing in the foreground the activated sludge tanks in which aeration is controlled automatically (Source: Water Pollution Research Laboratory, Stevenage, England)

Adaptive Radiation   Diversification of a group of organisms into subgroups which spread in various directions and into various environments *q.v.*; or, the phenomenon of distantly related organisms evolving similar ecological tolerances, and hence occupying similar niches *q.v.* in similar habitats *q.v.*

Adiabatic Process   A process in which heat does not enter or leave the system. Adiabatic processes play a fundamental role in meteorology *q.v.*, e.g. if a parcel of air rises it expands against a falling environmental pressure, the work of expanding being at the expense of its internal energy resulting in a fall in temperature, despite the fact that no heat leaves the parcel.

Adjustment   A behavioural response of organisms as a result of experience, resulting in internal changes to the social organization or in movement to a different situation.

Aerator   A device for introducing air into a liquid, either submerged (perforated pipe) or surface (mechanical paddles).

See Sewage Treatment.

Aeroallergens Vegetable dust and pollen suspended in the air which cause allergic diseases such as hay fever.

Aerobic Living or active in the presence of free oxygen; an aerobic process is one taking place in the presence of free oxygen. A state in which oxygen dissolved in water acts as an oxidizing agent. This is the normal condition of a healthy river, the rate of cleansing depending on the concentration of the dissolved oxygen *q.v.* available.

See Anaerobic.

Aerosol A particle of solid or liquid matter of such small size that it can remain suspended in the atmosphere *q.v.* for a long period of time; aerosols diffuse light, and the larger particles settle out on horizontal surfaces or cling to vertical surfaces. All air contains aerosols, the larger particles above 5μ in size being filtered out in the nose or bronchia. The smaller particles below 5μ in size pass into the lungs; they may be expelled immediately or retained for varying periods of time. Aerosols are classified into smoke, fumes, dust and mists.

Aetiology The science of the investigation of the cause or origin of disease.

Aggradation The building up of land by the deposition of material, e.g. by the deposition of detritus by streams where they flow over a surface of reduced gradient.

Air Mass Formed in the troposphere *q.v.*, a vast body of air having fairly uniform meteorological characteristics. Air masses are comparable in size with continents, moving in one of the atmospheric currents of the general atmospheric circulation. Fronts are theoretical surfaces dividing one air mass from another. An air mass is designated by geographic origin as either continental or maritime, tropical or polar.

Air Pollution The contamination of the atmosphere *q.v.* with undesirable solids, liquids and gases. In a strict sense, air may be considered polluted when there is added to it any substance foreign or additional to its normal composition. This definition of pollution is much too wide, however, for the purposes of practical air pollution control,

Substances with known effects on health (acute or chronic)	Substances thought to have long-term effects per se [a]	Potential long-term effects of combinations
Arsenic	Arsenic (arsenical dermatitis)	
Asbestos	Asbestos (asbestosis, mesothelioma)	
Beryllium	Beryllium (berylliosis)	Be + F (fluorides potentiate pulmon-changes in berylliosis)
Carbon monoxide		Synergistic in pO_2 depression
Carcinogens		Carcinogens produce tumours in presence of promotors
Fluoride	Fluoride (fluorosis)	Fluoride (promotes or accelerates lung disease)
Hydrocarbons		HC + O_3 → tumorigen + influenza →cancer
Hydrogen sulfide (possibly with mercaptans)		Antagonizes pollutants (strictly speaking not detrimental to health)
Inorganic particulates	Inorganic particulates (pulmonary sclerosis)	
Lead		
Nitric Oxide		
Nitrogen dioxide	Nitrogen dioxide (mild acclerator of lung tumours)	NO_2 + micro-organisms (pneumonia) + HNO_3 (bronchiolitis, fibrosa obliterans) + tars (smoker's lung cancer)
Organic oxidants (peroxyacylnitrates)		
Organic particulates (asthmagenic agents)	Asthmagenic agents (asthma)	
Ozone	Ozone (chronic lung changes, accelerated aging)	O_3 + micro-organisms (lung-tumour accelerator)
Sulfur dioxide, sulfur trioxide		SO_2, SO_3 + particulates aggravate lung disease

a Effects are given in parenthesis.

Table 1   Air pollutants with recognized or potential long-term effects on health at usual air-pollution levels (Source: World Health Organisation, *Research Into Environmental Pollution*, Technical Report Series No. 406, Geneva: 1968)

and the term "air pollution" is usually restricted to those conditions in which the general atmosphere contains substances in concentrations which are harmful, or likely to be harmful, to man or to his environment. A fuller definition of American origin is — "substances present in the atmosphere in concentrations great enough to interfere directly or indirectly with man's comfort, safety or health, or with the full use or enjoyment of his property". In respect of health, this reiterates the dictum that there are no such things as toxic substances, only toxic concentrations. The concept of concentration cannot be divorced, however, from time or duration of exposure; or from the acute or chronic effects likely to arise from high short-term or low long-term exposures respectively.

While London smog has diminished under the impact of progressive measures, it is interesting to distinguish between this type of smog and that of Los Angeles, which is of photochemical origin.

Photochemical smog is significant in other American cities and in Tokyo, while some of the eastern state capitals of Australia, notably Sydney and Melbourne, have proved to be candidates for this affliction in the course of time. Undoubtedly, the use in technical literature of such an imprecise term as "smog", as well as its variants such as "smaze" and "smust", creates confusion. The interchange of the results of air quality investigations is being made easier, however, through the adoption of a common nomenclature, consistent metric units, and uniform methods; this process is, however, far from complete.

See London Smog Incidents, Los Angeles Smog; Self-Cleansing. *also* Table 1.

Aitken Nuclei   Small particles a few hundredths of a micron in diameter, which normally exist in the atmosphere *q.v.* in concentrations varying from a few thousand to a few hundred thousand per millilitre. They are produced in large number by most combustion processes.

Albedo   That fraction of incoming solar energy *q.v.* which is reflected directly without being absorbed, a measure of the reflectivity of the Earth.

Aldehydes   A class of chemical compounds intermediate

between alcohols and acids; most are colourless, volatile fluids with suffocating odours.

Aldrin A white insecticide containing a chlorinated derivative of naphthalene, $C_{12}H_8Cl_6$. It is especially effective against pests resistant to DDT *q.v.*

Algae Simple plants, containing chlorophyll *q.v.* and/or other photosynthetic pigments, found widely in water and other damp situations. Usually microscopic, these plants may be freely suspended or attached to surfaces. Component groups are classified on the basis of structure, pigments, flagella, and chemical nature of the cell wall. Algal growth is dependent upon the presence of a number of chemical elements in suitable proportions; these elements include phosphorus, nitrogen, carbon and many others. These nutrients are derived from a variety of sources; decay of natural vegetation, weathering of rocks including phosphorus deposits in some areas, human wastes, phosphate detergents, industrial effluents, and agricultural run-off.

See Eutrophication.

Alkyl Sulphonates (AS) Surface-active agents and basic components of synthetic detergents. Alkyl benzene sulphonate (ABS) is stable and resistant to biodegradation. The discharge of detergent residues containing ABS results in foaming of the receiving waters and interference with sewage treatment processes. Linear alkyl sulphonates (LAS) show much better biodegradability.

See Detergents.

Allelochemistry The study of secondary substances involved in interference occurring between two or more populations *q.v.*

Allelopathy Interference between populations involving the release of inhibiting chemicals.

Allopatric Populations *q.v.* with separate dispersal areas.

Alluvium Sediment transported by streams and deposited on land.

Alpha Diversity or niche *q.v.* diversification. Diversity occurring as a result of competition between species *q.v.* in more favourable environments; as a result the variation in individual species becomes more limited.

See Beta Diversity.

Alpha Radiation Particulate radiation, each alpha particle being a helium nucleus of high velocity; the particles have a relatively low penetrating power.

See Beta Radiation, Gamma Radiation.

Altruistic Term applied to traits which have been selected because of their effects on group rather than individual survival.

Alveoli Innumerable minute, air-filled sacs in the human lungs; they are thin-walled and surrounded by blood vessels. It is through their surfaces that the respiratory exchange of oxygen and carbon dioxide occurs.

See Bronchitis.

Ambient Quality Standards or environmental quality standards. Maximum permissible limits, maximum allowable concentrations, maximum acceptable levels of pollutants in specified media other than the receptor *q.v.* designed to ensure that under specified circumstances a primary or secondary standard *q.v.* is not exceeded.

Ammonification The reduction of nitrates and nitrites to ammonium compounds by soil saprobes (putrid bacteria).

Anabatic Wind or mountain wind. Caused by air being warmed by contact with the ground during day-time and flowing uphill. Opposite of a katabatic wind *q.v.*.

Anabolism A facet of metabolism *q.v.* relating to those changes involving the breakdown of foodstuffs and their rebuilding to form body tissues.

Anadromous Fish Fish, such as the salmon, which spends most of its growing years in the ocean and, after attaining sexual maturity, ascends freshwater streams in order to spawn. The erection of power and irrigation dams, or the presence of thermal pollution, may isolate considerable numbers of fish from their traditional spawning grounds.

Anaerobic Living or active in the absence of free oxygen; an anaerobic process is one taking place in the absence of oxygen. The remaining oxygen may be combined in the form of some organic or inorganic compound, e.g. nitrate or sulphate. If sulphate acts as an oxidizing agent, hydrogen sulphide *q.v.* is formed giving rise to objectionable odour. Sulphate-reducing bacteria, though present in rivers, are normally inhibited by the presence of dissolved or free oxygen.

See Aerobic.

Anaerobic Digestion   A digestion process which permanently removes the offensive odour of many organic wastes so that they can be utilized on agricultural land without causing nuisance. A high proportion of the chemical oxygen demand *q.v.* can be removed with the recovery of the organic carbon as methane *q.v.*, while most of the lipids *q.v.* and other constituents which otherwise might attract flies and vermin are degraded. The wide variety of bacteria involved in the process may be classified into two broad groups:

1. Acid-producers (non-methanogenic bacteria) which, together with their associated enzymes, degrade most types of organic material mainly into the lower fatty acids (acetic acid accounting for about 80 per cent of the total) with much smaller amounts of lower aldehydes and ketones;
2. Methane-producers (methanogenic bacteria) which convert the soluble products of the acid-producers into a mixture of methane and carbon dioxide *q.v.*

Anion   A negatively charged ion of an electrolyte which migrates towards the anode under the influence of a potential gradient.

Anode   The electrode of an electrolytic cell at which oxidation occurs. Usually, in corrosion processes, it is the electrode that has the greater tendency to go into solution.

Anomaly   A deviation from uniformity; a geological feature considered capable of being associated with commercially-valuable hydrocarbons *q.v.* or minerals.

Anoxia   A deficiency of oxygen, e.g. in the tissues or in the blood, or in a body of water. In the Baltic, anoxic bottom-water conditions tend to persist in the deeper parts.

Antagonistic Effect   The tendency of some chemicals and processes to react together to form combinations which may have a less powerful effect than the substances or processes taken separately, opposite of a synergistic effect *q.v.*. The term is also applied where the growth of one organism is inhibited by another through the creation of unfavourable circumstances, e.g. by exhaustion of the food supply.

Antibiotic   A secondary biotic substance secreted by an organism which inhibits growth in other organisms.

Anticyclone   A high pressure area with winds rotating clockwise around the centre in the northern hemisphere and anti-clockwise in the southern hemisphere. There is a general slow descent of air over wide areas. In summer an anticyclone generally means fine, warm, sunny weather; in winter however dense sheets of stratocumulus cloud may be formed under high-pressure influences giving conditions known as "anti-cyclonic" gloom; as the air descends it is compressed and heated so that a deep inversion *q.v.* layer is formed, often resulting in fog.

See also London Smog incidents.

Application Factor   The ratio between the concentration of some substance producing a selected chronic response and that causing 50 per cent mortality in 40 to 168 hours. From this may be derived the concept of the "safe application factor", i.e. that fraction of the lethal level of substance that would be environmentally safe for the organisms concerned.

See Incipient Lethal Level.

Aquiclude   A geological formation of rock or soil which, although porous and capable of absorbing water slowly, will not transmit it fast enough to furnish an appreciable supply for a spring or well.

Aquifer   A geological formation or porous soil *q.v.* through which water may percolate for long distances, perhaps very slowly, yielding ground water to springs and wells. The contamination of aquifers with industrial wastes may lead to the pollution of water supplies.

Aquitard   A geological formation of rock or soil which retards the movement of ground-water. *q.v.*

Arboreal   Relating to trees; hence an arborist is a person who studies trees, and arboriculture is concerned with forestry and the culture of trees.

Arthropoda   A phylum *q.v.* of invertebrate animals with jointed limbs and a body divided into segments; the body generally is covered with a chitinous shell. The largest group in the animal kingdom in number of species, it includes crustaceans, insects, spiders, centipedes, and related forms.

Artificial Reef   A method of solid waste disposal, which comprises the tipping into deep water of junk and debris, rusting car bodies, used car tyres, and other material. The reef provides cover and breeding sites for various marine fish. The method has been used to advantage in New York City and San Francisco, without apparent detrimental effects.

Asbestos A broad term embracing several fibrous minerals with chrysotile, a hydrated magnesium silicate, being the most common form. Asbestos fibres may enter the general environment from the activities of asbestos cement industries and from the abrasion of brake linings in motor vehicles. Occupational exposure may cause specific chronic lung disease (asbestosis *q.v.*) while inhalation of asbestos by the general population may be a possible additional factor in the incidence of lung disease along with other air pollutants and smoking. Inhalation of asbestos has also been associated with mesothelioma (a rare form of cancer.)

Asbestosis A disease of the lungs caused by the inhalation of asbestos particles; sufferers are particularly liable to develop cancer of the lungs.

Association A conceptual grouping of populations in a community *q.v.* characterized by particular dominant species *q.v.*

Atmosphere The gaseous envelope of air surrounding the earth, the principle constituents of which are nitrogen and oxygen in proportions by volume of about 79.1 per cent and 20.9 per cent respectively. Carbon dioxide *q.v.* is also present to the extent of about 0.03 per cent, together with very small amounts of inert gases such as argon, krypton, xenon, neon and helium. Also present are water vapour, traces of ammonia, organic matter, ozone, salts, and suspended solid particles.

See also Greenhouse Effect; Meteorology.

Attribute Sampling Sampling in which the characteristic determined is simply a quality or attribute.

Australasian Region The biogeographical region comprising Australia, New Zealand, New Guinea, some eastern Indonesian Islands and some Pacific Islands.

Autotrophic Descriptive of organisms which synthesize organic from inorganic substances.

B

Backing Wind The anti-clockwise change of direction of a wind, e.g. from N through NW; an opposite change of direction to veering. The same definition applies whether in the northern or southern hemisphere.

See Meteorology.

Bacteria A large group of unicellular or filamentous microscopic organisms, lacking chlorophyll *q.v.* and multiplying rapidly by simple fissure. Bacteria occur in air, water, decaying organic material, animals and plants.

See Coliform Bacteria.

Bag Filter A device for removing particulate matter from the waste gases of industrial processes. The filter medium is a woven or felted fabric usually in the form of a tube. The bags may be up to ten metres in length and up to one metre in diameter. The upper ends are closed, while their lower ends are connected to a gas inlet which also serves as a hopper to catch the dust which is shaken down from the bags by mechanical or air reversal methods. The collecting efficiencies of bag filters are high, between 99 and 99.9 per cent; low gas velocities of the order of 1 to 3 m/min are required. The choice of materials for bag filters is limited by temperature limitations, being:

a) wool or felt 90° C

b) nylon, 200° C

d) glass fibre, siliconized and graphite impregnated for longer life, 260° C.

Plants have been constructed at British and American power stations to appraise the suitability of bag filters for power station emissions.

Battersea Gas Washing Process A method of wet-scrubbing the flue gases from the coal-fired Battersea power station, located in London on the Thames, to remove large quantities of sulphur dioxide *q.v.* The washing medium comprises water from the Thames with the addition of chalk. About 35 tons of water are required for each ton of coal burnt. The efficiency of removal of sulphur dioxide is of the order of 95 per cent. The effluent is discharged into the river as an almost saturated solution of calcium sulphate. A similar system is used at Bankside power

station, also situated in London on the Thames, where oil containing 3 to 4 per cent sulphur is consumed. The process has several drawbacks:
1. the plume is cooled and the residual sulphur dioxide and moisture fall readily on to the surrounding district
2. the sulphur is not recovered in a useful form
3. enormous quantities of water are required and water pollution occurs
4. it promotes corrosion problems and adds significantly to generating costs.

Beef Cattle Feedlot An area to hold a high concentration of cattle in pens or enclosures for a period of time. These are fattened by intensive feeding, rather than by grazing. All feed is stored, processed and distributed to the cattle. Beef cattle feedlots are a potential hazard to the environment because of the volume of wastes generated which require extensive waste disposal and utilization systems. The quality of water in streams, ground waters and catchment areas may be degraded. Wastes may also cause degradation of the land and plants to which they are applied. Noise, dust and odours may also present a nuisance.

Behaviour The manner in which living organisms respond to stimulation, sometimes called ethology. The behavioural activities of organisms may be grouped into three kinds:
1. the accommodation *q.v.* of the individual population *q.v.* within the habitats of the ecosystem *q.v.* in which it is found
2. the regulation of individual interactions within the population, or social behaviour
3. reproductive behaviour to maintain the population.

Beneficial Use A use of the environment *q.v.* or any element or segment of the environment that is conducive to public benefit, welfare, safety, or health, and which requires protection from the effects of waste discharges, emissions, deposits, and despoilation. Beneficial uses include:
1. Potable water supply for drinking, domestic and municipal purposes
2. agricultural and industrial water supply
3. habitats for the support and propagation of fish and other aquatic life

4. recreational activities such as bathing, fishing and boating
5. scenic and aesthetic enjoyment
6. navigation
7. wildlife habitats.
   See also Residual Use.

Benthos   Animals and plants living on the bottom of a sea or lake, attached or unattached, from the deepest levels up to the high-water mark. Benthic organisms are divided into littoral *q.v.* and deep water organisms.

Benzpyrene   A hydrocarbon *q.v.* present in coal and cigarette smoke, strongly suspected of being carcinogenic (cancerous) to man.
   See Carcinogenic Compounds.

Berylliosis   A disease of the lungs caused by the inhalation of particles of beryllium oxide.

Beta Diversity   or habitat *q.v.* diversification. Diversity occurring as a result of competition between species, thus revealing an increasingly narrow range of tolerance of environmental factors.
   See Alpha Diversity.

Beta Radiation   Radiation consisting of highvelocity negative electrons. Their ionizing power is far less than that of alpha particles, but their penetrating power is greater.
   See Alpha Radiation, Gamma Radiation.

Bilharziasis   or Schistosomiasis. A parasitic disease of humans caused by infection with a genus of blood-flukes comprising *Schistosoma mansoni, S. japonicum* and *S. haematobium*. Regarded as one of the major public health problems in certain parts of the world, notably parts of Africa, Central and South America, and Southern and Eastern Asia, Bilharziasis is commonly transmitted by bathing in polluted canal water; an increase of irrigation favours its spread. The intermediate host of the worm is the fresh-water snail. The cercaria (larval form) of the fluke enter the host (man) through the skin; the infection gives rise to severe disease of the urinary tract, liver and lungs, which is often fatal. The maturation of the worms in the human system leads to the excretion of eggs; on passing to water the cycle is repeated.

Bioassay   The determination of the character and strength of a potentially toxic compound by studying its effects on standard test organisms under laboratory conditions. This is often determined in the form of the median tolerance limit (TL_m), defined as the concentration of toxicant or substance in which 50 per cent of the test organisms survive for a given time. This may be expressed also as the dose level lethal to 50 per cent of the test organisms (LD_{50}). For convenience, the 24-hour TL_m or the 96-hour TL_m may be determined.

Biochemical Oxidation The process by which micro-organisms within an aerobic *q.v.* treatment process transform organic pollutants into settleable organic or inert mineral substances.

Biochemical Oxygen Demand (BOD) The weight of oxygen taken up mainly as a result of the oxidation of the constituents of a sample of water by biological action. The result is expressed as the number of parts per million (or grammes per litre) of oxygen taken up by the sample from water originally saturated with air, usually over a period of 5 days at a temperature of 20° C. The result gives some measure of the amount of biologically degradable organic material in polluted waters, although when samples contain substances such as sulphites or sulphides, which are oxidized by a purely chemical process, the oxygen so absorbed may form part of the BOD result. The BOD test is no longer an adequate criterion for judging the presence or absence of pollution for many relatively new pollutants must be considered, e.g. pesticides, industrial organic compounds, fertilizing nutrients, dissolved salts, soluble iron and manganese, and heat.

Biocide Any agent that kills organisms.

Biocoenology A study with the object of deriving from an analysis of complex associations, an understanding of the numerical determination of species. Synonymous with synecology.

Biodegradable Readily decomposed by bacterial activity. Soaps are readily decomposed shortly after discharge into a sewerage system. Earlier synthetic detergents of the alkyl-benzene-sulphonate (ABS) type were non-biodegradable, possessed high foam stability and remained intact sometimes for years. Subsequently, the detergent industry changed to linear alkylate sulphonate which is more amenable to the decomposing action of bacteria.

Biogeochemical Cycles   The pathways of nutrients through ecosystems *q.v.*
   See Calcium Cycle, Carbon Cycle, Cellular Respiration, Nitrogen Cycle, Phosphorus Cycle, Sulphur Cycle.

Biogeographical Regions *See* Australasian Region, Ethiopean Region, Nearctic Region, Neotropical Region, Oriental Region, and Palaearctic Region.

Biological Bench-mark   A concept in which animals and plants are used to measure pollution, either instead of or to augment the physico-chemical studies traditionally employed. Bench-marks of population levels and fitness are required against which future changes can be evaluated.

Biological Control   The use of natural agents to control pests and other problems, e.g. the control of prickly pear in Australia using the cochineal insect *Dactylopius ceylonicus* and the larvae of the moth *Cactoblastis cactorum*; the control of rabbits using the virus myxomatosis; and in an instance in the United States, the planting of marigolds to allow the excretion from their roots to kill soil nematodes. Control agents may be used in combination; this type of biotic activity is termed "biosynergistic", the combined effects of different biotic agents greatly exceeding the effect of the agents considered singly. Not all biological control measures are successful. The Cane Toad, *Bufo Marinus,* was introduced to control the insect pests of sugar-cane; it was released in the area between Cairns and Tully, North Queensland, in 1935. By 1945, the insects were as numerous as ever and cane damage had not decreased.

Biological Monitoring   The direct measurement of the changes in the biological status of a habitat *q.v.*, e.g. to determine variations in the composition and abundance of biota *q.v.*, above and below an effluent outfall, or before and after the commencement of a potentially detrimental waste discharge.

Biological Shield   A thick wall or shield, usually consisting of a three to four metre thickness of concrete, surrounding the core of a nuclear reactor to absorb neutrons and gamma radiation *q.v.* for the protection of operating personnel.

Biomass   The total weight of all living matter in a particular habitat *q.v.* or area. Biomass is often expressed as grams of organic matter per square metre. Biomass differs from productivity which is the rate at which organic matter is created by photosynthesis *q.v.*
See Gross Productivity.

Biome   A community *q.v.* of plants or animals extending over a large natural area; a major regional ecological community such as a tropical rain forest *q.v.*

Biometeorology   Studies involving pollutants and infectious agents, and the interaction of pollutants and weather factors.
See Meteorology.

Biosphere   The sphere of living organisms (plants and animals, including microorganisms); it comprises parts of the atmosphere, the hydrosphere, (oceans, inland waters and subterranean water) and the lithosphere. The biosphere includes the human habitat *q.v.* or environment *q.v.* in the widest sense of these terms.

Biostimulants   Substances which stimulate the growth of aquatic plants. For example, the addition of large amounts of nitrogen and phosphorus compounds to lakes may stimulate massive growth of microscopic plants such as blue-green algae or the larger water-weeds. The process is called cultural eutrophication.
Sewage is a major source of biostimulants, particularly nitrogen and phosphorus. A large part of the phosphorus found in sewage is derived from domestic and industrial detergents *q.v.* which contain phosphorus compounds to enhance their cleaning properties.

Biosystematics   The study of the biology of populations, particularly in relation to their breeding systems, reproductive behaviour, variation and evolution.

Biota   The animal and plant life found within an environment *q.v.* or a geographical region.

Biotic   Relating to life and living systems, rather than the physical and chemical characteristics of an environment *q.v.* Biotic factors are influences in the environment that emanate from the activities of living organisms.
See Abiotic.

Biotic Element   The organisms which form the populations and communities within an ecosystem *q.v.*

Biotic Potential The maximum potential capacity for growth likely to be exhibited by a population *q.v.*

Biotope A region of relatively uniform environmental conditions occupied by a given plant community and its associated animal community. The interdependent biological and physical components are in equilibrium if their relative numbers remain more or less the same, forming a stable ecological community or system.

Black Smoke Smoke produced when particles of carbon are derived from the cracking of hydrocarbon gases, following sudden cooling. Smoke is visible evidence of incomplete combustion.

    See also Brown Smoke, Smoke.

Blow-by Gases consisting of carburetted gasoline together with some exhaust products which blow past the piston rings into the crankcase of an internal combustion engine. For many years American-made automobiles utilized a system of crankcase ventilation employing a road draft tube. With this system, air flowing past the moving vehicle aspirated crankcase fumes through the tube from the crankcase. Replacement air was drawn through a combination oil filter cap and air inlet. Devices to control crankcase emissions became mandatory in California from 1961 onwards. Control has consisted in returning crankcase ventilation air and gases to the engine intake manifold for consumption during operations. The negative pressure of the engine induction system is used to establish a positive flow of the crankcase ventilation air through the crankcase. This technique, now compulsory on all new Australian cars, has solved about 25 per cent of the hydrocarbon *q.v.* emission problem of the passenger car; other hydrocarbon emissions emanate from the exhaust and from the carburettor.

Bottom Load Material transported by running water, being rolled or pushed along the bottom of the watercourse.

Brigalow Forest A term embracing a wide range of vegetation of which the dominant tree is brigalow, *Acacia harpophylla*, growing between 9 and 15 metres in height. A programme for the clearing of large areas of Brigalow land was launched by the Queensland Government in 1961 with the aim of increasing the beef cattle carrying capacity of the land, by planting improved pasture species. It has been claimed that the beef carrying capacity will have increased five-fold when the project is completed. The programme has caused concern to those interested in animal and plant conservation.

Bronchiolitis Inflammation of the bronchioles (one of the terminal sub-divisions of the bronchia of the lungs).

Bronchitis Inflammation of the mucous membrane of the bronchial tubes existing in either an acute or chronic form. Epidemiological studies have indicated that there is a correlation between high concentrations of air pollution and morbidity and mortality among chronic bronchitics, although the ultimate progress of this disease is sensitive, particularly in winter, to many stimuli of which air pollution is but one. Despite the complexity of the problem, the British Medical Research Council has concluded that cigarette smoking and air pollution are two important factors in the causation of the disease.

Brown Smoke Smoke produced by tarry volatile matter given off from coal at relatively low temperatures.
See also Black Smoke; Smoke.

Burn Up The amount of the fissile material in a nuclear reactor which is destroyed by fission or neutron capture, expressed as a percentage of the original quantity of fissile material present. Alternatively, the heat obtained per unit mass of fuel, expressed generally as MW/days tonne. In nuclear reactors using metallic uranium fuel elements in advanced gas-cooled reactors, an average burn-up of 18,000 MW/days tonne is expected.
See Nuclear Reactor.

C

Cadmium A heavy metal, occurring in the rare mineral greenockite CdS and in association with zinc ores. A painful malady known as the itai-itai or ouch-ouch disease afflicted the residents of the Japanese town of Fuchu in the Toyama Prefecture north-west of Tokyo over some twenty years. The ailment gave rise to sudden sharp twinges of pain in various parts of the body causing the victim to cry out "itai" (the Japanese word for "ouch"). More than 100 deaths were attributed to the malady over the period.

Following a two year study by a special research team of the Japan Public Health Association, the blame was eventually attached to water pollution. According to an official report by the Ministry of Health & Welfare, the painful malady was the result of absorbing excessive amounts of cadmium, into the system over a large period of time, causing the bones to become brittle. Responsibility was placed on a mining company whose waste from a cadmium mine polluted the Jintsh River which flows through Fuchu. The company had already been paying compensation to farmers along the river for damage to their crops.

Calcium Cycle The circulation of calcium atoms brought about mainly by living things. Thus calcium is taken up from the soil by trees and other plants and deposited in roots, trunks, stems and leaves. Rain may leach some calcium from the leaves and return it to the soil. Creatures such as insects, rabbits, and other herbivores *q.v.* obtain their share of calcium from the plants and leaves; birds acquire it by eating the insects. Animals and birds die, leaves and branches fall and decay, and thus the calcium component returns to the soil. Some calcium may be lost from an ecosystem *q.v.* by leaching and surface run-off *q.v.* carried to bodies of water; it is recycled through phytoplankton *q.v.*, zooplankton *q.v.*, fish, and lake and ocean water. Sea spray taken up to the atmosphere and airborne dust return calcium to the land. In a balanced ecosystem, gains equal losses.

See Biogeochemical Cycles.

Carbamates Selective nonpersistent alkaloid insecticides that act through cholinesterase inhibition; includes carbaryl or Sevin.

See Pesticides.

Carbon Cycle The circulation of carbon atoms brought about mainly by living things. Organic carbonaceous matter in rivers and other bodies of water is derived from domestic and industrial effluents, animals and plants, and soil erosion. Such carbonaceous matter is oxidized to carbon dioxide by aerobic bacteria thriving in the presence of dissolved oxygen. Carbon dioxide released may be neutralized in whole or part by basic elements present (e.g. sodium, calcium, or magnesium) to bicarbonates or carbonates. The process is analogous to respiration in animals in which oxygen is absorbed and carbon dioxide released. The reverse process, the production of oxygen from carbon dioxide, is carried out by chlorophyll-containing (green) plants only in the presence of bright sunlight (photosynthesis). The carbon is utilized for the synthesis of complex organic compounds (e.g. fats and carbohydrates) and the oxygen released. In the absence of dissolved or free oxygen, anaerobic bacteria metabolize organic compounds (putrefaction) resulting in the production of methane. This process occurs in septic tanks and sewage sludge digestion tanks as well as in deposits of sludge, mud and vegetation.

See Biogeochemical Cycles.

Carbon Dioxide A colourless gas produced when carbon is burned in a sufficient supply of oxygen to complete the reaction $C + O_2 \Rightarrow CO_2$. It is present in flue gases to a varying extent, but in typical cases amounts to 12 per cent of the total volume of gases present. If the supply of combustion air is insufficient, carbon monoxide *q.v.* is formed. Carbon dioxide is a normal constituent of the atmosphere to the extent of about 0.03 per cent by volume.

See Greenhouse Effect

Carbon Monoxide An invisible, tasteless, odourless and highly poisonous gas. It burns with a pale blue flame to form carbon dioxide *q.v.* and results from the incomplete combustion of carbonaceous materials. It is found in many industrial works, in the exhaust gases from internal combustion engines and in smoke from chimneys. Carbon monoxide has an affinity for the haemoglobin of the blood three hundred times that of oxygen and readily forms carboxyhaemoglobin *q.v.* in the red blood corpuscles. As the red blood corpuscles cannot carry their full quota of oxygen to the tissues of the body, the tissues suffer from oxygen starvation and show the symptoms of "carbon monoxide poisoning".

Carboxyhaemoglobin (COHb) A combination of carbon

monoxide *q.v.* and the respiratory pigment occurring in the blood plasma, haemoglobin. The haemoglobin is deprived of its oxygen-exchanging properties, with resultant poisoning and suffocation of the body. Haemoglobin, while having a marked affinity for oxygen to form oxyhaemoglobin, has an even greater affinity for carbon monoxide. Individuals absorb carbon monoxide as smokers, from the emissions of petrol-driven vehicles, and sometimes from occupational exposure. A normal and non-smoking person, breathing air devoid of carbon monoxide, will have blood containing about 0.4 per cent COHb; this is called the "background COHb level".

Carcinogenic Compounds Complex chemical compounds producing cancer in experimental animals and strongly suspected of contributing to lung cancer in man. One of the best known carcinogens is 3,4 benzpyrene. In 1933, Cook and co-workers, with the assistance of fluorescence spectroscopy, isolated from two tons of pitch a substance characterized by synthesis as 3,4 benzpyrene; it is now known that coal tar contains about 1.5 per cent of the carcinogen. In recent years, benzpyrene and other carcinogenic hydrocarbons have been identified in soot, carbon black, processed rubber, the exhaust gases of gasoline and diesel engines, coal gas, coffee soots, smoked food, and cigarette and tobacco smoke. Relatively large concentrations of some carcinogenic hydrocarbons have also been found in the atmospheres of some cities. Some of the complex polycyclic hydrocarbons formed in smoke have been shown to be carcinogenic when applied to the skin of animals. Coal tar and certain petroleums become carcinogenic only after being heated.

Carcinoma Alternative name for cancer.

Carnivore An animal or plant feeding on, and digesting, animal substances as a source of food.
  See Herbivore, Omnivore.

Carp *See* Rough Fish.

Carrying Capacity The population size or steady state population at which some limiting factor or substance, or a combination of these, prevents further population increase: an important concept when considering optimum population size. The carrying capacity represents the point of balance between reproduction potential and environmental resistance.

See Brigalow Forest.

Catabolism   A facet of metabolism *q.v.* relating to the breakdown of tissues accompanied by the release of energy.

Catadromous Fish   A fish which spends most of its growing years in freshwater and, after attaining sexual maturity, descends to the ocean in order to spawn. The catadromous American eel (*Anguilla bostoniensis*) descends the New England streams when sexually mature, swims hundreds of miles to a site in the Sargasso Sea east of Bermuda, spawns in deep water and dies. The larvae float to the surface and migrate northwards, transported partly by the Gulf Stream, and eventually ascend the New England freshwater streams.

Catchment   A region or drainage basin which collects all the rainwater that falls on it, apart from that removed by evaporation, directing it into a river or stream which then carries the water to the sea or to a lake. The boundary of a catchment basin is defined by the ridge beyond which the water flows in the opposite direction, i.e. away from the basin.

Cellular Respiration   A complex biochemical process which breaks down the carbohydrates produced by photosynthesis *q.v.* (either in the plants themselves or in the animals that eat them). Cellular respiration is a slow combustion or oxidation process and the chemical energy thus liberated is used by the plants or animals for their living functions. The end products of cellular respiration are carbon dioxide and water which are returned to the atmosphere, completing the cycle of carbon dioxide.

See Biogeochemical Cycles.

Cesspool   A storage tank for sewage; it should be watertight and should not be allowed to overflow. When full, it should be emptied in a nuisance-free manner with the safe disposal of the contents elsewhere.

See also Septic Tank.

Chemical Mutagens   Sources of mutations, other than radiation, which may give rise to mutations resulting in an increase in the incidence of congenital defects in future generations. Mankind is being exposed to many thousands of synthetic chemicals whose mutagenic potential is unknown.

Chemical Oxygen Demand (COD) The weight of oxygen taken up by the total amount of organic matter in a sample of water without distinguishing between bio-degradable and non-biodegradable organic matter. The result is expressed as the number of parts per million (or milligrams per litre, or grams per cubic metre) of oxygen taken up from a solution of boiling potassium dichromate in two hours. The test has been used for assessing the strength of sewage and trade wastes.

Chlordane A chlorinated hydrocarbon insecticide; it is a viscous, volatile, amber-coloured liquid.

   See Chlorinated Hydrocarbon Insecticides.

Chlorinated Hydrocarbon Insecticides A diverse group of persistent synthetic chemical poisons; the group includes aldrin, dieldrin, endrin, heptachlor, and DDT. The chlorinated hydrocarbon compounds tend to remain unchanged for many years in soil, river mud, and marine sediment. The half-life *q.v.* of DDT is 10 to 15 years, i.e. at the end of that period half the original amount of DDT still remains unchanged. In a further period of 10 to 15 years, one-quarter of the original amount would still persist. In contrast, the organo-phosphorus pesticides have a "total life" ranging from a few days to less than a year. The organo-chlorine pesticides can be toxic to fish, reptiles, birds, mammals, crabs and molluscs. Pesticides present in small amounts in water can concentrate many times over in the various links in the food chain. Although fish may not themselves be killed at the lower levels of pollution, their bodies may contain sufficient pesticide residue for the ingestion of them to harm or kill the birds which feed on them.

   See Pesticides.

Chlorination The use of chlorine for the treatment of water; a practice which has spread steadily throughout all parts of the world. In waterworks, chlorination is used to kill bacteria *q.v.* and for the removal of algae *q.v.* growth, iron, manganese, and sulphides. In swimming pools also it is used to control bacterial contamination, inhibit algae growths and improve water quality. In power generation, the chlorination of condenser cooling water helps to control slime-forming bacteria and to eliminate fouling by mussels, thus maintaining condenser efficiency. In sewage treatment works, chlorination may be used to improve final effluent quality. In the food processing industries, the chlorination of retort cooling water helps to prevent spoilage and blown cans; chlorinated water also helps to reduce carcase contamination in meat and poultry processing factories. Chlorination also ensures a wholesome water supply in dairies and ice-cream factories, and for bottle-washing plants in breweries and soft-drink plants. The effective sterilization or disinfection of water by the application of chlorine requires the constant presence of a "chlorine residual"; that is, free chlorine remaining in the water after a necessary period of contact, otherwise chlorination may give a false sense of security, particularly in water of varying organic content. Frequent and reliable estimations of the chlorine residual are necessary.

Chlorine Demand   The amount of chlorine required by any given volume of sewage or polluted water to kill all pathogenic bacteria q.v. therein.

Chlorophyll   The composite green pigment of plants.

Clarification   The removal of settleable and floating solids from sewage q.v.

Claus Kiln   An oil refinery unit for the recovery of sulphur from hydrogen-sulphide-rich gases. Hydrogen sulphide is burned in an insufficient supply of oxygen for complete combustion, the principle of preferential combustion giving the reaction:
$$2H_2S + O_2 \Rightarrow 2H_2O + 2S$$

Climate   The average weather conditions of a place or region throughout the season. It is governed by latitude, position in relation to continents or oceans, and local geographical conditions. Near the equator, climate is almost synonymous with weather q.v. due to the more stable conditions. It is described in terms of atmospheric pressure, temperature, solar radiation, wind speed and direction, cloudiness, humidity, rainfall, evaporation, incidence of fog and temperature inversions, lightning and thunderstorms, visibility, and other characteristics.

See Meteorology.

Climax Plant Community A plant community that maintains itself, more or less unchanged, for a long period of time under natural conditions, i.e. it is in equilibrium. Interference with a climax community through the side-effects of human settlement (e.g. logging, grazing, burning) results in a different plant community known as a disclimax community.

Coastal Protection Measures to prevent coast erosion including the stabilization of beaches and dunes by mechanical means in the lower parts of the beaches, and by both mechanical and vegetational means on the upper beaches and dunes. Heavy sea walls and revetments may also be used in appropriate cases.

Groynes are used extensively to slow beach erosion and to build beaches. Made of wood or other material, and designed to take advantage of the long-shore currents that carry the sediments along the beach, Groynes are usually developed in a series so that their spacing, length and height, form a tapering system.

Natural vegetation has been the most effective measure in stabilizing dunes and upper beaches; the vegetation may consist of herbs, shrubs and trees. Wattles, fences and stakes may be used in conjunction with plantings to inhibit the movement of sand. The planting arrangements are related to the topography, wind, and drift-character of the sands. The problem of dune management is complex.

See Littoral Drift, Sand-Mining.

Cochlea A tiny snail-shaped structure forming the inner ear. The ossicles of the middle ear transmit the vibrations to a fluid contained in the cochlea within which are microscopic hair cells that move back and forth in response to sound waves. It is the energy impulses created by the movement of these crucial hair cells that go to the brain, where they are interpreted as sound. The hair cells can be damaged either temporarily or permanently, by intense sound waves. Those seemingly most susceptible to damage are those that respond to the high frequencies; such selective damage can severely impair the understanding of human speech.

Coliform Bacteria   Bacteria *q.v.*, including the bacterium *Escherichia Coli*, commonly found in the human large intestine and whose presence in the environment usually indicates contamination by human wastes. Laboratory results are expressed as the number of organisms per 100 ml of sample. While the presence of *E. Coli* indicates faecal pollution, the organism is generally considered to be non-pathogenic. To confirm that pathogenic organisms *q.v.* are associated with faecal pollution, samples should be tested for the pathogenic genera *Salmonella* and *Shigella*. If *Salmonella* is detected, further tests are needed in order to differentiate between the organisms of this group, e.g. *Salmonella Typhosa* is the causative organism of typhoid fever, whereas *Salmonella Typhimurium* is the causative organism only of gasto-intestinal upsets.

There are other coliform bacteria more or less similar to *E. Coli* that exist in soil and plant materials (particularly *Aerobacter Aerogenes* and *Escherichia freundii*); they may be present in water without indicating faecal pollution.

Colloidal Particles   Material that is in a very fine state of division: particles will not settle out or pass through a semipermeable membrane.

Combined Sewer   A single conduit or pipe intended for the removal of sullage, sewage and storm-water, as distinct from a separate system in which the storm- and rain-water is removed through a separate conduit.
    See Sullage Water.

Commensals   Two or more kinds of organisms that live together, with one or several benefitting and without injury to any.

Comminutor   A primary treatment *q.v.* process for sewage combining screening with the grinding of large solids, the shredded material being returned to the sewage.

Commons, Tragedy of the   A tragedy of overgrazing and lack of care which resulted in erosion and falling productivity of the English commons, prior to the enclosure movement when grazing rights became restricted to the few. At one time each community had its commons, set aside for public use and used essentially for sheep and cattle grazing. Eventually the number of animals became more than the commons could support, and no one had any interest in ensuring the future productivity of this resource. Exploitation continued until productivity collapsed, and this social institution was superseded. Today, on a larger scale, the natural resources of air and water may be regarded as the 'commons' of the world; they are exploited by many who have no interest in the future productivity of these resources. Hence, for example, intensive fishing and whaling threaten a dramatic loss of productivity — a repeat of the tragedy of the commons.

See also International Whaling Commission.

Community In ecology *q.v.*, any naturally occurring group of different organisms sharing a particular habitat *q.v.*, interacting with each cther particularly through food relationships while being relatively independent of other groups.

Composting A biological process in which the organic material in refuse *q.v.* is converted to a usable stable material by the action of micro-organisms present in the refuse. A composting plant can range from a simple windrowing of raw refuse until it is broken down — then screening of the material to remove rejects, to a sophisticated, fully mechanical operation. In a modern plant, the refuse is fed into a digester where the refuse is broken up and commences its conversion to compost. After a period that may range up to five days, the refuse is fed through pulverizers and screened. The reject material is normally carted away to tips whilst the fine material is windrowed for several months, the windrows being turned periodically. Some plants pulverize the refuse initially and then windrow the screened material. It is quite common to add sewage sludge in the plant to serve as an additive to the compost and, of course, to dispose of the sludge. A compost plant will produce about 45 per cent compost from the refuse treated.

Compost from refuse is a soil conditioner with some manurial value, but it is not a fertilizer in itself. It adds humus to the soil and helps break up the structure of the soil, improving the moisture-retaining properties.

Compression The compaction of refuse *q.v.* under high pressure into blocks or cubes weighing in the region of five tons or more; the resultant blocks are bound with

bitumenized fabric, plastic or sheet metal, and either transported to tip sites or used as filling material for reclamation works or shore protection works. By compression the
volume of refuse is reduced by about 75 to 80 per cent.

Concretion A solid or concrete mass of matter formed by
coalescence or cohesion.

Coning Description applied to a plume when it is expanding
roughly along a cone. Chimney plumes do this when either
efflux momentum or buoyancy or both are dominant in
determining the path of the plume.

Confluence The point at which one stream or river flows
into another, or where two streams or rivers converge and
unite.

Conservation The rational use of the environment *q.v.* to
improve the quality of living for mankind. Rational use
implies:

1. The use of some areas and resources for production to
   satisfy the requirements of humanity for goods and
   services
2. The preservation or enhancement of other areas and
   resources for the contribution these can make to the
   scientific, educational, aesthetic, or recreational requirements of mankind. For the community as a whole,
   marginal costs should be balanced against marginal
   benefits over the whole scene of productive, cultural,
   and recreational ativities, the interests of both present
   and future generations being taken into account. Such
   balancing often becomes a difficult and controversial
   matter, e.g. lake preservation versus electricity generation; the destruction of high value forest land to make
   room for some marginal extension of grazing land; the
   sacrifice of park land for mining; the deployment of low
   lying land for housing versus the risks of flood damage;
   population growth versus congestion; land reclamation
   versus the retention of mangroves. Conservation is not
   therefore incompatible with development, in the
   traditional sense, but raises difficult issues to be settled
   outside of the market place.
   See also Economic Conservation, Human Progress
   Index, Land-Use, Nature Conservation, Quality of Life,
   Soil Conservation, Structural Conservation, Sustained
   Yield Conservation.

Consumption Residues Wastes arising from the consumption of final goods and services.

See also Production Residues.

Contamination A condition or state of the water environment which represents a health danger (particularly to humans) because of the presence of live pathogenic bacteria *q.v.* or toxic materials.

Continental Shelf A comparatively shallow zone that borders the continents and separates them from the deeper oceanic regions; shelves exhibit a wide range of variation, particularly in size, depth, width, topography, and gradient. A shelf has been commonly accepted as the area between the 183-metre line (100 fathoms) and the continental shoreline. In few parts of the world does a natural break occur at this precise depth; hence the use of the 183-metre line is an arbitrary one. The continental shelves of the world range from narrow fringes less than eight kilometres wide to enormous submarine plains up to 1,000 kilometres in width; a shelf is thus a complex, variable zone. The Australian shelf occupies an area of approximately 2,600,000 square kilometres, i.e. equal to one-third of the land area. South of the tropic, the shelf is mostly less than 80 kilometres wide, while in the tropical regions it may exceed 300 kilometres in parts. The shelf-edge depths range from about 73 metres (40 fathoms) to 165 metres (90 fathoms).

See Continental Slope.

Continental Slope That portion of the continental margin beginning at the outer edge of the continental shelf *q.v.* and descending to greater depths.

Contour Farming Ploughing, seeding, cultivating and harvesting across the slope rather than with it. Ploughing is horizontal, following the curvature of the hills with every furrow acting as a reservoir to retain water. Siltation, a common cause of water pollution, is also reduced.

See Soil Erosion Control.

Contour Strip Cropping The planting of crops on contour strips as an effective erosion deterrent. Crops are alternated along the contours. Strip cropping is combined frequently with crop rotation.

See Soil Erosition Control.

Controlled Tipping   *See* Land-Fill.

Conurbation   An area which is occupied by a mass of streets, factories, commercial premises, and dwellings, while possibly enclosing small isolated rural localities, formed by the growth of several neighbouring and formerly separate towns, e.g. the Birmingham conurbation of England.

Cooling Pond   A large tank of water in which irradiated fuel elements from a nuclear reactor are stored to allow the short-lived fission products to decay. Also an artificial lake used for the natural cooling of condenser-cooling water serving a conventional power station; examples are to be seen at Swanbank power station in Queensland and Hazelwood power station in Victoria.

Cooling Tower   A device for cooling water by evaporation in the ambient air. A tower requires a flow of air and this may be induced by natural or mechanical means. The use of large cooling towers at power stations to dissipate recovered waste heat eliminates the problem of thermal pollution *q.v.* in masses of water; however, the make-up water for a cooling tower system is taken from the river or stream, thus eliminating its subsequent use down-river. After being used several times for cooling purposes, it is finally dissipated to the general atmosphere as steam. *See* Figure 13, p. 162.

Coriolis Force   The apparent force caused by the earth's rotation which serves to deflect a moving body on the surface of the earth clockwise in the northern hemisphere, but anti-clockwise in the southern hemisphere.

Cosmic Rays   A complex, very penetrating system of radiation incident upon the Earth from outer space.

Cost-benefit Analysis   A systematic comparison between the cost of carrying out a service or activity and the value of that service or activity, quantifying as far as possible all costs and benefits whether direct or indirect, financial or social. Where public services are involved this comparison is of particular value and relevance because both cost and benefit to the general public are evaluated; thus a public service may be justified in circumstances which a private organization would regard as 'uneconomic'. While the cost of damage is a direct charge to the community, the cost of control is indirect, it being assumed that costs incurred by industry will be met by the community through higher prices. Without control, the cost of air pollution to the community is extremely high; with a high degree of control this cost is minimized though not eliminated.

The cost of industrial devices and techniques varies from zero up to a point where little or no additional benefit to the community is gained from additional expenditure. The figure suggests that a sensible balance between costs and benefits is achieved when the total costs of damage and control are minimized. Although actual cost-curve shapes in any given situation are by no means necessarily as shown, are also very difficult to construct and are valid for only a short period of time (say one to five years), the concept is useful.

Cost-benefit Ratio   A ratio calculated:

$$\frac{\text{Gross Benefits (present value)}}{\text{Gross Costs (present value)}}$$

The gross costs and benefits are discounted over the life of the project by a selected annual rate of interest. The difference between the two amounts is the present value of net benefits. The ratio of the two amounts is the gross cost-benefit ratio. Both considerations are relevant in choosing between projects.

Costs of Pollution   The social costs and penalties imposed on a community or population that are not recorded in the accounts of polluters. Various monetary estimates of the losses have been made, all of them of a high order of magnitude. The British Committee on Air Pollution, under the chairmanship of Sir Hugh Beaver, reported in 1954 that the economic cost of air pollution in Britain, taking into account many direct and indirect costs but excluding the cost of medical services, was of the order of £250 million per year. Subsequently, in the Foreword to Gilpin's *Control of Air Pollution* (1963) Sir Hugh Beaver presented a revised total figure of £400 million per year. The United States Environment Protection Agency has estimated that the average annual cost of air pollution is about $65 per person, or a total for the nation of about $13,000 million (13 billion dollars). Pollution control proposals being implemented in the United States of

America between 1970 and 1980 represent an increase from just under one per cent to a little over two per cent of actual and prospective Gross National Product (G.N.P.) *q.v.* Data on the estimated costs of fighting pollution in thirteen countries have been published by the Organization for Economic Co-operation and Development (O.E.C.D.). They indicate that in the framework of present environmental objectives overall costs of pollution control of all kinds may not exceed three per cent of G.N.P. during the 1970s. Pollution control costs are not evenly distributed throughout the economy and some branches of industry are more affected than others.

Counter An instrument which records, as a number, a certain fraction of the total individual disintegrations occurring in a source of radioactivity during a given time.

Creode The pattern of development of the single living organism from the fertilized egg to its final death and dissolution.

Criteria Scientific requirements on which a decision or judgment may be based concerning the suitability of a resource (e.g. water) to support a designated use.
See Beneficial Use.

Critical Links Organisms in the food chain *q.v.* of a particular community *q.v.* which are responsible for energy capture and flow and for nutrient assimilation and release. These are essential for the preservation of the health of the ecosystem *q.v.* and are in general abundant and widespread sediment dwellers.

Critical Organ An organ to which special attention is paid in considering the effects of radiation upon the human body, either because of its property of selectively concentrating within itself a specific radioisotope, or because of its radio-sensitivity.

Crop Rotation A technique of planting different crops at different seasons to avoid exhausting the soil in respect of one kind of nutrient or exhausting the ground-water *q.v.* at any one given level.

Crown-of-thorns Starfish *(Acanthaster planci)* A multi-armed starfish, reaching a size of 60 cm diameter, that has caused extensive damage to coral between the latitudes of Cairns to Townsville. The first report of *Acanthaster planci* on the Reef was in 1921, but no large concentrations were noticed until 1964. A Committee which reported to the House of Representatives in 1971 expressed the opinion that *Acanthaster planci* did not constitute a threat to the Great Barrier Reef as a whole, but indicated an urgent need for more research. Controversy arose on this issue because of differences of opinion in respect of actual and potential damage to the Reef, the nature and cause of the apparent increased numbers of starfish, and the methods of control to be adopted. The starfish, which prefers a hard coral as food, is found also in association with coral reefs in tropical waters in the Indian and Pacific oceans.

Crustaceans Animals, mostly aquatic, with a hard, close-fitting shell which is shed periodically:— includes lobsters and crabs.

Crystalline Rock Rock consisting of minerals in an obviously crystalline state, usually of igneous *q.v.* and metamorphic *q.v.* origin.

Culm and Gob Banks Inferior fuel and waste of no commercial value discharged from coal-processing plants on to land where it accumulates into hills or banks of culm (anthracite) and gob (bituminous). These banks visually disfigure the landscape and are often easily ignited, either from an external source of through spontaneous combustion.

Cultch Materials (such as oyster shells and pebbles) dumped into the sea to furnish places of attachment for the larval stage of the oyster (or any other shellfish).

Cultural Eutrophication *See* Biostimulants.

Curie The unit of radioactivity *q.v.* It is equal to that quantity of any radioactive nuclide in which the number of disintegrations per second is 3.7×10^{10}.

Cyanides The salts of hydrocyanic acid which are virulent poisons. The objections to cyanides in effluents are as follows:

1. The toxic effects which they have on fish and other life in rivers, and on bacteria in sewage works
2. Their ability to absorb oxygen
3. The formation of extremely poisonous hydrogen cyanide gas which can endanger the lives of persons working in sewers.

In some areas a significant contribution is made to the toxicity of rivers by cyanides derived from metal finishing processes such as electro-plating, cleaning and case-hardening, or from the scrubbing of coke-oven or blast furnace gas. River authorities often set an upper limit for cyanides in river water of 1 ppm; sewerage authorities may set an upper limit of 10 ppm. Cyanides may be removed from an effluent by oxidation with chlorine to produce cyanates which are relatively harmless, or by precipitation of the cyanides as a complex iron cyanide after treatment with lime and ferrous sulphate.

Cyclodiene Insecticides A subgroup of the chlorinated hydrocarbons, including chlordane, heptachlor, aldrin, dieldrin, and endrin.

See Chlorinated Hydrocarbon Insecticides.

Cyclone

1. A device for removing particulate matter from the waste gases of industrial processes. A simple cyclone consists of a cylindrical upper section and conical bottom section. The dust-laden gases enter the cylindrical section tangentially. Centrifugal action throws the grit and dust particles to the outer walls; these particles fall by gravity to the dust outlet at the bottom. The relatively clean gases leave through a centrally situated tube within the upper section. With a suitable pressure drop, separation of particles down to about 40 μ can be achieved. Cyclones may be used singly, or in groups or nests.

2. In meteorology *q.v.*, a low pressure area with winds rotating counter-clockwise around the centre in the northern hemisphere, and clockwise in the southern hemisphere. Winds bring in moisture and rainy, windy weather prevails as rising air cools and vapour condenses.

See Anticyclone.

Cytotype A member of a population *q.v.* composed of individuals with essentially similar karyotypes *q.v.*, which differ from those of individuals in other populations.

D

D.D.T. Abbreviation for the chlorinated hydrocarbon insecticide dichlorodiphenyl trichlorethane, a synthetic product remarkable for its high toxicity to insects at low rates of application and for the persistent effectiveness of its residual deposits. This latter characteristic, however, has had some unfortunate effects, particularly when D.D.T. has become concentrated in passing through the food chain *q.v.* At Long Island Sound, U.S.A., mosquito-infested marshes were sprayed with D.D.T. Initially, D.D.T. was found in low concentrations of about 0.000003 ppm, but it accumulated to:

> 0.04 ppm in plankton
> 0.50 ppm in plankton eating fish
> 2.00 ppm in larger fish
> 25.00 ppm in fish-eating birds

This is almost a 10^7 multiplication of the original residue. In the United States, there has been a steady decline of predatories such as the Bald Eagle, Osprey and Peregrine Falcon whose prey accumulate D.D.T.

D.D.T. has been found to induce the synthesis of hepatic enzymes able to hydroxylate estrogen and other steroid sex-hormones. The results can be both profound and unpredictable. Estrogen levels may be depressed or elevated; the best known effect is through the estrogen-controlled calcium metabolism which has led to birds laying much thicker or thinner eggshells than usual.

D.D.T. is virtually insoluble in water, but it is very soluble in lipids such as fat; it tends to end up in the fatty reserves and liver of contaminated animals. The insecticide has been found in several large rivers of the United States in concentrations of from 1 to 20 parts per thousand million parts; in the United Kingdom, quantities detected have amounted to only about 1 part per thousand million. Several countries have severely restricted the use of D.D.T. Australia has prohibited the spraying of dairy pastures with D.D.T., as it cannot be used without producing a high residue in butterfat products. Suitable alternative insecticides are available to control pests without producing persistent residues, e.g. malathion and other organophosphorus compounds. The U.S. Food and Drug Administration has severly restricted the permitted levels of D.D.T. in meat for human consumption.

See also Chlorinated Hydrocarbon Insecticides.

Decibel A (dBA) Scale An international weighted scale of sound levels which attenuates the upper and lower frequency content and accentuates middle frequencies, thus providing a good correlation in many cases with subjective impressions of loudness and sense of annoyance. Nearly all audible sounds lie between 0 and about 140 dBA, O dBA is the 'threshold of hearing', while sounds above about 140 dBA are not common. An increase of 10 dBA means that the noise perceived by a listener has roughly doubled in loudness. A car passing at 70 dBA sounds twice as loud as one passing at 60 dBA. The dBA measurement is widely used throughout the world for determining approximate human reaction to noise, and is the basis of legislation to control noise in many countries. Examples of typical dBA levels are as follows:

	dBA
Rustle of leaves	10
Quiet office	50
Busy office	65
Moderate traffic	70
Alarm clock ringing	80
Very noisy factory	90

Declaration on the Human Environment A declaration of common outlook and common principles issued at the conclusion of the United Nations Conference on the Human Environment held at Stockholm, Sweden, from 5—16 June 1972. The full text is published as an appendix to this Dictionary.

Decomposer An agent of decomposition, e.g. heterotrophic *q.v.* organisms in an ecosystem which obtain energy from the breakdown of dead organic matter.

Decomposition The separation of organic material into simpler compounds.

Deforestation The removal of forest and undergrowth to increase the surface of arable land or to use the timber for construction or industrial purposes. Forest and its undergrowth possess a very high water-retaining capacity, inhibiting run-off of rain-water. Removal gives rise to rain-fall erosion which takes on several forms:

1. Sheet erosion which occurs on flat ground and washes away the superficial layer of soil with a high content of humus
2. Rill erosion on broken ground when the water runs down along the lines of the steepest gradient
3. Gully or ravine erosion which is often a later and aggravated phase of rill erosion causing the formation of ravines
4. Sliding or slip erosion in the form of landslides, stone falls and subsurface erosion.

Not only is the water regime drastically modified but there are also climatic changes.

See Rill, Soil Conservation, Soil Erosion, Soil Erosion Control.

Deme A segment of a population *q.v.* in which there is no natural barrier to interbreeding.

Demersal Refers to fish that live on or adjacent to the sea-bottom.

Demographic Transition A fundamental change in the characteristic trends of a population *q.v.*, e.g. a transition from high birth rates and low death rates, to low birth rates and low death rates. Much of Europe and North America has passed through this demographic transition. Japan is now experiencing the same transition characteristic of the Western world; the growth rate of the population of Japan has declined to about one per cent per annum, similar to that of North America.

See Population Explosion.

Demography The study of population dynamics *q.v.*; when related to human populations, the characteristics measured include the size of a population and its distribution by age, sex, occupation, industry, location, etc., together with the trends in these characteristics.

See Population Explosion.

Density Dependent Description applied to population *q.v.* regulatory mechanisms which are controlled or influenced by the size of the population; the term 'density independent' is applied to population regulatory mechanisms which are not controlled or influenced by the size of the population.

Design Rule A system whereby manufacturers are required to design their products so that certain noise level or emission level requirements are satisfied, e.g. Australian Design Rules No. 26 and No. 27 relating to restrictions on the emissions from the exhausts of new passenger cars, which came into force on 1 January 1972, and 1 January 1974 respectively.

Detention Period The average amount of time that each unit volume of liquid or gas is retained in a tank or chamber in a flow process. A minimum detention period is essential to complete a given stage of the process, e.g. the destruction of certain classes of bacteria, or the settlement of certain size fractions of solid particles.

Detergents Surface-active agents, capable of removing dirt and grease from a variety of surfaces. The synthetic household detergents that began to be marketed some twenty-five years ago contained, as their principal component, an alkylbenzene sulphonate (a molecule comprising a benzene nucleus to which was attached a sodium sulphonate graph and an alkyl chain containing usually eight or more carbon atoms). This type of surface-active material proved particularly resistant to decomposition by bacterial action, unlike soaps which undergo rapid decomposition. As a consequence of this resistance to bacterial attack, the early alkylbenzene sulphonates were only partially decomposed during the treatment of sewage and about half the quantity originally present was subsequently discharged with the sewage effluent. The foaming that occurred when detergent residues reached surface waters is well known. Through impeding the rate at which oxygen could be transferred from the gas phase to solution, these substances not only raised the cost of sewage treatment but also tended to inhibit the processes of self-purification in watercourses. The only practicable solution was to develop substitutes more susceptible to bacterial attack. It was found that if the alkyl side chain was straight instead of branched, resistance to bacterial decomposition was greatly reduced. Manufacturers of synthetic detergents in Britain decided, as from 1 January 1965, to replace the original non-degradable 'hard' anionic detergents by biologically 'soft' materials. A similar substitution took place in the United States of America and Australia.

Apprehension has also been expressed about the use of phosphates in detergents as 'builders' which not only economize in the use of the relatively expensive surfactant materials but increase the effectiveness of those reactants. Phosphates from many sources play a crucial role in accelerating the processes of eutrophication *q.v.* of lakes and water-ways. It was suggested at one stage that nitrilotriacetic acid (NTA) could provide a substitute builder in detergents but this possible substitute presented its own environmental problems. As yet no satisfactory substitute for the sodium tripolyphosphate in domestic detergents has emerged.

Dialysis The filtration of substances through semipermeable membranes.

Diastrophism The process by which the Earth's crust is deformed, e.g. by bending, folding, and breaking.

Diatom Unicellular algae having cell walls impregnated with silica that persists as a skeleton after death; forms a large proportion of plankton *q.v.* in both sea-water and freshwater.

Dieldrin A white crystalline insecticide, $C_{12} Cl_6 H_8 0$, produced by oxidation of aldrin. It has a high contact and stomach toxicity for most insects. Skin contact, inhalation, and food contamination should be avoided. Dieldrin belongs to the chlorinated hydrocarbon group. It has been suggested that a drop in the breeding rate amongst Golden Eagles in Scotland was linked with the introduction of dieldrin into sheep-dips and the simultaneous occurrence of dieldrin in unhatched eggs. Dieldrin sheep-dips were banned in 1966; since then dieldrin levels in eggs have dropped and the Golden Eagle breeding rate has gone back to normal.

See Chlorinated Hydrocarbon Insecticides.

Diffusion The spreading or scattering of a gas or liquid, or of heat or light. In air pollution *q.v.* studies of the general atmosphere *q.v.*, molecular diffusion is ignored, its effect being insignificant when compared with that of turbulence.

Digestion The conversion of organic material into simpler chemical compounds through the action of enzymes *q.v.* produced by living creatures.

Dilution   A form of effluent disposal in which relatively small volumes of effluent are discharged into large receiving bodies of air or water.

Disclimax Plant Community   *See* Climax Plant Community.

Disinfection   The destruction of pathogenic organisms *q.v.*, usually by the application of chlorine.

   See Chlorination.

Disintegration   The disruption of the nucleus of an atom with the ejection of an alpha or beta particle.

   See Alpha Radiation, Beta Radiation.

Dissolved Oxygen   The amount of oxygen available for biochemical activity within a given volume of water expressed as milligrams per litre, grams per cubic metre, or parts per million by weight. The saturation point depends upon the temperature, barometric pressure, and the chemical characteristics of the water. The amount of dissolved oxygen in water is of vital importance to living organisms. In normal conditions water is saturated when it contains about 10 ppm oxygen at $0°C$. As the temperature of the water rises the solubility of oxygen decreases, so that at $20°C$ and $30°C$ water is saturated at about 6.5 ppm and 5.5 ppm respectively. A rise in temperature also increases the rate of solution of oxygen from the air. Nevertheless, under constant conditions, the level of oxygen will fall to a lower value in hot than in cold weather.

   In still water, oxygen entering at the surface can only pass into a region of lower concentration by diffusion; in those circumstances diffusion is an extremely slow process. The rate at which oxygen diffuses into a body of water diminishes with increasing depth. In running water, however, turbulence will distribute the oxygen much more rapidly; the rate of solution in a swift flowing stream may be two hundred times as great as that in nearly stagnant water. The greater the turbulence the greater is the rate of solution of oxygen from the air.

   After discharge, organic substances are oxidized by bacterial action, withdrawing oxygen from solution in the water. The organic pollutant is described as placing a "demand" on the oxygen in a river. The extent to which the level of dissolved oxygen will fall depends upon the rate of oxidation and the rate of re-aeration.

When the flow of a river is at its lowest (the "dry weather flow"), the oxygen concentration is also likely to be lowered as a result of sluggish water movement. Simultaneously, the concentration of pollutants may be high through diminished dilution.

See Figure 2.

Figure 2   Submersible device (known as a Store Unit) for measuring and recording dissolved oxygen and temperature in rivers and other bodies of water (Source: Water Pollution Research Laboratory, Stevenage, England)

District Heating   A scheme in which both heat and hot water are provided from a central boiler plant to an entire housing estate or group of buildings; the consumer enjoys house heating at a comfortable level and a constant supply of hot water. There are two types of district heating scheme:

1. combined electric power and heating plant in which steam is bled from a high pressure turbine to a water heater
2. central boiler plant specially designed and constructed for the district heating scheme.

The scale of the scheme and the density of the premises to

be served are of great importance to the economics in a particular case. Also known as block heating (a scheme serving one or two blocks of flats or a shopping centre) and as group heating (a scheme serving a group of buildings or small housing estate). Environmentally, the combustion of fuel takes place in the most efficient manner at one point, with the best facilities for dealing with the products of combustion; many individual point sources of pollution are thus displaced.

Diurnal Daily, or recurring every day; the diurnal cycle of air pollution *q.v.* concentrations is of great interest to air pollution control agencies.

Diversification An increase in the variation exhibited by a population *q.v.* or community *q.v.* over time.

Domestic Sewage Wastes consisting of human bodily discharges carried by flushing water; sullage water *q.v.* from kitchens, bathrooms and laundries; and other water-borne material discarded as a result of regular household and human sanitary activities.

Dominance In ecology *q.v.*, the phenomenon in which energy flowing through an ecosytem *q.v.* moves preferentially through a limited number of populations; in sociology, the imposition of a hierarchy in a population *q.v.* which determines or influences the ability of individuals to gain access to the rewards of society, and perhaps to essential requirements. The group of individuals which has established itself in the highest position in a social hierarchy is known as a "dominance clique".

Donora Smog Incident An air pollution *q.v.* episode occurring in Donora, Pennsylvania, in October 1948, involving morbidity and mortality. An industrial town, Donora is situated in the valley of the River Monongahela, in hilly country, 48 kilometres south of Pittsburgh, U.S.A. The valley is about one and a half kilometres wide, the sides rising to some 120 metres above the river. Heavy industries in the valley have included many steel and blast furnaces, steel mills, smelting works, sulphuric acid plant, and other works. Soft coal is the primary fuel.

Visible smog until 10 a.m. has been the rule at Donora; in spring and autumn this commonly persists throughout the day, and even for several days. During the period

25–31 October 1948, very stable weather conditions produced effects closely similar to those in the Meuse Valley incident of 1930, with the fog accumulating day by day until it was terminated by rain on 31 October. About 42 per cent of the total population of 14,000 suffered some illness, 10 per cent being seriously ill.

Eighteen deaths resulted, all in persons over fifty years of age, with fourteen of these persons having had a previous history of respiratory illness. The final conclusion of the investigators was that no single substance was responsible for the episode, but that the toxic effects could have been produced by a combination or summation of the action of two or more contaminants. Sulphur dioxide and its oxidation products, together with particulate matter, were considered to be significant contaminants.

Doubling Time In demography *q.v.*, the period of time during which a population *q.v.* density doubles.

Down-Draught A region of severe turbulence formed on the leeward side when wind flows around and over a building. The region of down-draught begins at the top of the windward face of the building, rises to about twice the height of the building, and stretches for about six times the height of the building downwind. Chimney emissions discharged into a down-draught zone will be brought rapidly to the ground. Chimneys should discharge their gases high enough for them to escape the influence of down-draught. A Committee appointed by the British Electricity Commissioners recommended in 1932 that a power station chimney should be at least two-and-a-half times the height of the tallest adjacent building (usually the power station boiler house), plus an allowance for any difficult topographical features in the vicinity. Today, some chimneys may need to be higher than this to ensure the adequate dispersal of sulphur dioxide. The two-and-a-half times rule may be relaxed in respect of buildings less "cliff-like" in shape than power station buildings.

See Down-Wash.

Down-Wash The drawing down of chimney gases into a system of vortices or eddies which form in the lee of a chimney when a wind is blowing. Down-wash affects the visual appearance of the plume and causes blackening of the stack. In extreme circumstances, it may also assist in bringing flue gases prematurely to ground level. To overcome the risk of frequent down-wash it is necessary to discharge the gases from the mouth of the chimney at a sufficiently high velocity. Gases may be discharged from modern power station chimneys at a velocity of 80 kilometres per hour.

See Down-Draught.

Drainage Basin *See* Catchment.

Dry-Weather Flow The sewage *q.v.*, together with infiltration, if any, flowing in a sewer in dry weather; or the rate of flow of such sewage.

Dual-Purpose Sewer A sewer which conveys both foul sewage and surface-water *q.v.*

Dunes *See* Coastal Protection, Littoral Drift, Sand Mining.

Dust Burden The weight of dust suspended in a unit of medium, e.g. flue gas. This may be expressed in grams per cubic metre at normal temperature and pressure.

Dynamometer A machine for measuring the brake horsepower of a prime mover, and used also in connection with test cycles for assessing emission rates from the exhausts of motor vehicles.

E

Earth Resources Technology Satellite (ERTS) An unmanned earth-orbiting satellite equipped to scan the surface of the earth and obtain many kinds of information relating to natural resources and the global environment *q.v.* The satellite (ERTS-1) was launched into space in July 1972, aboard a two-stage rocket, from the Vandenburg Air Force Base at Lompoc, California. ERTS-1 was designed to obtain information during its limited life valuable in agriculture, forestry, oceanography, geology, geography, ecology, and meteorology. The satellite was developed under the auspices of the U.S. National Aeronautics and Space Administration.

Earthwatch Programme A programme of global environmental assessment to assess trends in air, water, land, and human health; part of the Action Plan adopted by the United Nations Conference on the Human Environment *q.v.* in 1972. The programme includes a scheme for the establishment of ten baseline stations remote from all sources of pollution in order to monitor long-term global trends in atmospheric constituents and properties which may cause changes in meteorological properties, including climatic changes. Subsequently a much larger network of not less than 100 stations is to be set up for monitoring purposes on a regional basis to measure changes in the distribution and concentration of contaminants. The work is co-ordinated by the World Meteorological Organization.

Ecocline The directional variation in the characteristics of a population *q.v.* or community *q.v.* along an ecological gradient.

Ecological Niche *See* Niche.

Ecological Pyramid A grouping of the successively diminishing trophic levels of an ecosystem *q.v.*

See Trophic Level.

Ecology The study of ecosystems. The relationships between living organisms, and between them and their environment *q.v.* Ecology is concerned frequently with general principles that apply to both animals and plants. Autecology is concerned with single organisms or species, and synecology with communities of species, although these artificial partitions are no longer accepted by all ecologists. Human ecology is the study of the structure and development of human communities and societies in terms of the processes by which human populations adapt to their environments; as a subject it represents an application of the perspectives of the biological sciences to the investigation of topics included in the social sciences.

See Ecosystem.

Economic Conservation Conservation *q.v.*, the main purpose of which is the maximum sustained production of food, fibre and other useful plant materials; a concept of sustained yield. Economic conservation and nature conservation *q.v.* do not necessarily go hand-in-hand.

Economic Efficiency The efficiency with which scarce resources are used and organized to achieve stipulated economic ends. In competitive conditions, the lower the cost per unit of output, without sacrifice of quality, in relation to the value or price of the finished article, the greater the economic efficiency of the productive organization. The social worth of economic efficiency weakens in circumstances in which reduced costs of production are not reflected in lower prices to consumers, in real terms, and in circumstances in which social costs must be borne which are larger than the reduction in the recorded or accountancy costs of the productive organization.

Economic Ends   The objectives of economic activity; ends are both quantitative and qualitative, but with the nature of ends economic science has no direct concern. Economics is concerned only with the number of ends and with their degree of relative intensity. Economic ends form only a part, albeit a very important part, of the full spectrum of public and private objectives. Furthermore, the pursuit of economic ends in the short term may not be wholly acceptable economic ends to a community in the long term.

Economic Growth   The growth per head of population in the production of goods and services of all kinds to meet final demands, e.g. goods and services for domestic consumption, capital goods for accumulation, export goods to pay for imports. An acceleration of economic growth requires as much emphasis on such elements as better management, better training of labour and improved education, as upon higher capital investment. Furthermore, the quality of investment may count almost as much as the quantity. Capital investment, though important, is but one significant factor in the growth rate of an economy. The 'growth rate' is the annual growth, usually expressed as a percentage over the previous year, of productive capacity in a community; in assessing the growth rate per head, an adjustment must be made for changes in population.

Economic Problem   The problem of allocating scarce means to plentiful but competing ends. The boundaries of the "economic problem" coincide neither with the market economy nor with that part of the output of the economic system defined as the Gross Domestic Product *q.v.* Economic decisions, both public and private, cover a wider

Economic System, Functions of   The essential functions to
be fulfilled in the economic arrangements of any
community; these functions may be defined as follows:
1. Generally, to match supply to the effective demand for
goods and services in an efficient manner
2. to determine what goods and services are to be
produced and in what quantities
3. to distribute scarce resources among the industries
producing goods and services
4. to distribute the products of industry among members
of the community
5. to provide for maintenance and expansion of fixed
capital equipment
6. to fully utilize the resources of society.
In a free enterprise system, the fulfilment of these six
economic functions is left to the profit motive and the
price mechanism working within a framework of social
safeguards. In a socialist society all the operations required
are consciously planned by official organizations. Many
countries operate a mixed economy, splitting the economy
into public and private sectors, the activity of the whole
being influenced by direct and indirect planning measures.
All systems have tended to neglect the increasing abuse of
'free goods' such as air and water, as these social costs have
not fallen within the accountancy systems normally maintained. The increasing concern expressed in recent years in
respect of environmental effects has found reflection in
the policies of all countries, irrespective of political
complexion.

Economic Welfare   Defined by the Cambridge economist
A. C. Pigou (1877–1959) as "that part of social welfare
that can be brought directly or indirectly into relation
with the measuring rod of money"; in other words, those
aspects of social welfare which are concerned with material
as distinct from bodily, moral or spiritual well-being,
although obviously these are inter-related in some ways.
Pigou stressed that there is no precise line between
economic and non-economic satisfaction. Economic or
material satisfactions are derived from the consumption of
both goods and services; and it is this which is the subject
matter of economics. Pigou warned that economic welfare

will not serve for a barometer or index of total welfare; this is because an economic cause may affect non-economic welfare in ways that cancel its effect on economic welfare. Non-economic welfare is liable to be modified by the manner in which income is earned and also by the manner in which it is spent — "Of different acts of consumption that yield equal satisfactions, one may exercise a debasing and another an elevating influence."

See Marginal Social and Private Net Products.

Ecosphere That portion of the earth which includes the biosphere *q.v.* and all the ecological factors which operate on the living organisms it contains.

Ecosystem A natural complex of plant and animal populations and the particular sets of physical conditions under which they exist; the organisms of a locality, together with the functionally-related aspects of environment *q.v.*, considered as a single entity. The word 'ecosystem' is derived from two words 'ecology' and 'system'; the 'eco' part of the word implies environment, while the 'system' part of the word implies an interacting, interdependent complex. The word 'ecosystem' appears to have been coined by A. G. Tansley in 1935 in an article in the journal *Ecology* entitled 'The Use and Abuse of Vegetational Concepts and Terms'.

Ecotone or edge. Where two vegetation associations join, e.g. between rainforest and woodland or grassland. Some animals find their greatest abundance at the edge or ecotone, while some are restricted to it.

Ecumenopolis The universal city, the logical consequence of unlimited population growth. A term attributable to C. A. Doxiadis who defined fifteen different space units of increasingly greater dimensions starting with man himself and finishing with the ecumenopolis. Beyond the large city, Doxiadis traced logical development through the metropolis, conurbation, megalopolis *q.v.*, urban region, urban continent, and ecumenopolis, the all-encompassing universal city.

See Population Explosion.

Edaphic Of or pertaining to soil, especially with regard to its influence on plants and animals.

Eddy A current of air or water moving contrary to the main current or stream, especially one having a rotary or whirlpool motion.

Eddy Diffusion The process by which gases diffuse in the atmosphere; molecular diffusion is extremely slow by comparison and is usually ignored.

Effective Height of Emission The height above ground level at which a plume of waste gas is estimated to become approximately horizontal. It is usually higher than the height of the chimney due to the upward momentum and buoyancy of the gases.

Effluent The liquid, solid, or gaseous products discharged by a process, treated or untreated.

Effluent Charge A fixed fee levied by a regulating body against a polluter for each unit of waste discharged into public waters. The fee may be uniform for all waste producers in the area, or it may be selective according to the composition of individual wastes or the local absorption capacity. The fee may be charged continuously at all times, or it may be levied only when conditions deteriorate below a specified level.

Effluent Standard The maximum amount of specified pollutants allowed in discharged sewage as established by regulating agencies to achieve desirable stream standards. *See* Standard.

Egocentric Traits Traits which favour the survival of the individual organism.

Element In relation to the environment, means any of the principal constituent parts of the environment including water, atmosphere, soil, vegetation, climate, sound, odour, aesthetics, fish and wild life.

Emission Standard or effluent or discharge standard. The maximum acceptable release of a pollutant from a given source, to a specified medium under specified circumstances, e.g. the maximum acceptable release of sulphur dioxide by mass and concentration from a chimney of given height and diameter. *See* Standard.

Endangered Species Generally, fauna likely to become extinct due to vulnerability arising from pressure on highly specialized habitats, or direct exploitation by man, or threat from other species, or by a combination of inhibiting and destructive factors. Examples include the noisy scrub bird, Cape Barren goose, magpie goose, Burdekin duck, helmeted honeyeater, grey teal, bustard, emu, koala, New Holland mouse, mountain pigmy possum, leadbeater's possum, Cape York bandicoot, numbat, and dibbler (marsupial mouse).

Endemic   Belonging or native to a given geographic region; not introduced or naturalized.

Endothermic   In fuel technology, characterized by or formed with absorption of heat. The term is also applied to homeotherms, animals which maintain a constant temperature by physiological processes under internal control.

Endrin   A very toxic broad-spectrum insecticide and rodenticide.

   See Chlorinated Hydrocarbon Insecticides.

Enteric Bacteria   Bacteria that inhabit the intestines, including organisms that may cause infectious diseases such as typhoid.

   See Bacteria, Coliform Bacteria, Waterborne Diseases.

Energy Budget   A recording of the amounts of energy in relation to the several trophic levels *q.v.* of the populations in an ecosystem *q.v.*

Entropy   The measure of energy that is unavailable within a thermodynamic system. All energy used on Earth is ultimately dispersed and transformed into relatively low-temperature heat which is unavailable as energy; hence the consumption of fuels implies an irreversible increase of entropy and an increase in the temperature of the troposphere *q.v.*

Environment   The region, surroundings or circumstances in which anything exists; everything external to the organism. The environment of an organism includes:

1. the purely physical or abiotic milieu in which it exists, e.g. geographic location, climatic conditions, and terrain

2. the organic or biotic *q.v.* milieu including non-living organic matter and all other organisms, plants and animals in the region including the particular population *q.v.* to which the organism belongs.

The effective environment is everything external to the

organism which affects the fulfilment of that organism. Often, for the purposes of a particular study, the term environment is confined to factors external to a population; this practice creates a dichotomy, for the population under study is part of the environment of the individual creature within that population. The environment of the human being includes the abiotic factors of land, water, atmosphere, climate, sound, odours and tastes; the biotic factors of animals, plants, bacteria and viruses; and the social factor of aesthetics.

Environmental Forecasting A forecasting programme capable of timely and effective warning of technologically induced perturbations of any given health-welfare parameter of the population *q.v.* The need for environmental forecasting has grown with the pace of technological and community *q.v.* change. In making detailed forecasts concerning community hazards, models need to take account of emmision levels; the transport, storage and reaction of pollutants in the environment *q.v.*; and the resulting exposure of the community and its response.

Environmental Geology The application of geologic data and principles to the solution of problems likely to be created by human occupancy and use of the physical environment *q.v.*; geology oriented towards the planned utilization of resources and the safeguarding of the environment. The areas of interest include metallic and non-metallic minerals; mineral fuels; ground-water *q.v.*; soils and soil conditions unsuitable for septic systems or sanitary land-fill *q.v.* use; land use *q.v.*; and beach preservation.

Environmental Impact Statement A considered report, following careful studies, disclosing the likely or certain environmental consequences of a proposed action, thus alerting the decision-maker, the public and the government to the environmental risks involved; the findings enable better informed decisions to be made, perhaps to reject or defer the proposed action or to permit it subject to compliance with specified conditions. Each environmental impact statement must include:

1. A detailed description of the proposed action including information and technical data adequate to permit a careful assessment of environmental impact.

2. Discussion of the probable impact on the environment, including any impact on ecological systems and any direct or indirect consequences that may result from the action.
3. Discussion of any adverse environmental effects that cannot be avoided.
4. Alternatives to the proposed action that might avoid some or all of the adverse environmental effects, including analysis of costs and environmental impacts of these alternatives.
5. An assessment of the cumulative, long-term effects of the proposed action including its relationship to short-term use of the environment versus the environment's long-term productivity.
6. Any irreversible or irretrievable commitment of resources that might result from the action or which would curtail beneficial use of the environment.
7. Discussion of objections raised by government agencies, private organizations and individuals.

The impact statement procedure affords the public an opportunity to participate in decisions that may affect the human environment. The preparation or discussion of statements may involve the holding of public hearings or inquiries. Recognizing the need for broader consideration of environmental consequences at an early date, the Commonwealth Government and a number of States have enacted statutes or imposed conditions requiring environmental impact statements for major projects and other projects likely to have a significant environmental impact. This sifting of projects into those requiring impact statements and those which do not implies a measure of prejudging which in itself can be at times controversial. The alternative is a situation in which statements are required for all projects, throwing an enormous burden upon growing but not unlimited review resources. Impact studies carried out, or being carried out, in Australia include: Black Mountain PMG Tower, ACT., Brisbane Airport Development, Q., Illawarra Escarpment, NSW., Pollution from Kooragang Island, NSW., Natural Gas Pipeline, Moomba to Sydney. NSW., Newport 'D' Power Station, Vic., Yarra Brae Dam, Victoria.

Environmental Noise *See* Neighbourhood Noise, Noise.

Environmental Resistance The restriction of population *q.v.* growth through the interaction of one or more environmental factors.

Environment Protection That part of resource management which is concerned with the discharge to the environment of chemical and biological waste *q.v.* materials, and of physical effects (e.g. sound and radioactivity *q.v.*) with the aim of providing a defence against interference, damage, or destruction, in relation to those beneficial uses *q.v.* of natural resources *q.v.* valued by the community.

Enzyme A protein which functions as a catalyst (i.e. a substance which accelerates the rate of a chemical reaction, without itself being used up in the reaction), increasing the reactivity of a specific substance or group of substances (known as the substrate). Of many different kinds, enzymes promote the multitudinous reactions which take place in the living organism, e.g. the hydrolysis of fats, sugars and proteins, and their re-synthesis, and the many forms of oxidation and reduction which provide energy for the cell. Metabolism *q.v.* depends entirely upon enzymes, a very small amount producing a very great cumulative effect. Enzymes are susceptible, however, to a wide variety of substances which act generally as poisons; they may be destroyed and inactivated, for example, by insecticides.

Epidemiology A branch of medical science concerned with the study of the environmental, personal, and other factors that determine the incidence of disease. For example, epidemiological studies on large groups have shown that the prevalance of bronchitis is closely associated with air pollution and that mortality and morbidity varies closely with changes in smoke and sulphur dioxide. A deterioration in health of a group of 1,000 bronchitic patients was observed when smoke concentrations rose above 300 ug/m³ and sulphur dioxide above 600 ug/m³ (o.21 ppm). However, sulphur dioxide cannot be specifically incriminated since the concentrations of most pollutants rise and fall together; it is perhaps best regarded as an indicator.

Epilimnion The upper stratum of water in a lake which usually has the highest oxygen concentration and is characterized by a temperature gradient of less than one degree C per metre of depth.

Equilibrium Population A population *q.v.* that neither grows nor declines; in the absence of migration, the number of births in a given period must equal the number of deaths, a birth being defined as an entry into the population and a death a departure from it.

Eradication The complete and final extinction or extermination of a species throughout its range. Eradication programmes frequently fail in this absolute sense.

Erosion A process by which rock particles and soil are detached from their original site, transported, and then deposited at some new locality. The main agents of erosion are water and wind. Geological or natural erosion operates at an extremely slow rate; it is with accelerated erosion arising from the activities of man that the conservationist is primarily concerned. Soil erosion *q.v.*, can occur when land is cleared and cultivated; or when vegetation is destroyed by fire, overgrazing, or the development of conditions unsuitable for vegetation such as high salinity.

Escherichia Coli *(E. Coli)* *See* Coliform Bacteria.

Ethiopian Region The biogeographical region comprising Africa south of the Sahara.

Euphotic Zone The open water zone of the ocean, corresponding to the limnetic zone *q.v.* of a lake. The zone has sufficient sunlight to support photosynthesis *q.v.* and a considerable population of phytoplankton *q.v.* Usually, sunlight cannot penetrate deeper than 200 metres in most marine habitats; this depth is frequently considered the lower border of the euphotic zone. Below the euphotic zone lies the abyssal zone *q.v.*

Euryhaline *See* Stenohaline.

Eutrophic Rich in dissolved nutrients.
See Eutrophication.

Eutrophication The ageing of a body of water by the growth of vegetation, particularly algae *q.v.*; these plants flourish and then die, their decay using up the dissolved oxygen *q.v.* of the water with serious impairment of water quality. In lakes, rivers, harbours and estuaries, the accumulation of nutrients is a natural process. These nutrients include carbon, hydrogen, oxygen, sulphur, potassium, calcium, magnesium, nitrogen and phosphorus. Algal 'blooms', thriving on these nutrients, may be blue-green, red or brown in colour; in small numbers these plants are beneficial as they contribute to the oxygen balance in lakes and streams, and also serve as food for fish. Industrial and domestic activity may greatly accelerate an otherwise slow ageing process by increasing the amount of nutrients entering the water; effluents from these sources contain phosphorus and nitrogen. In addition, fertilizers containing phosphorus and nitrogen may be carried by rain-water run-off or ground-water seepage into lakes or streams.

The effects of advanced eutrophication are:
1. Lush algae create problems of water colour, taste and odour, resulting in increased costs of water treatment
2. the water is less attractive for boating, swimming and fishing
3. the more desirable types of fish may be eliminated
4. irrigation canals may become clogged.

Possible remedies include:
1. Removal of nutrients from waste waters, a very costly procedure
2. bypassing of lakes, diverting of waste waters to streams below the lake by pipeline
3. removal of excessive weeds and debris, and dredging of lake sediments
4. application of chemicals to destroy algal growths, copper sulphate and chlorine being commonly used for this purpose.

Other factors than nutrients influence the formation of algal blooms, including climatic, physical and chemical factors. Notable examples of accelerated eutrophication have been observed in lakes, flowing waters and reservoirs in almost all the more highly developed countries. Specific examples include Lake Erie; Lake Washington in Seattle, Washington; the Madison Lakes in Wisconsin; and Lake Zurich in Switzerland. In a developing country, Lake Tunis in Tunisia undergoes severe eutrophication during the summer months associated with the deaths of organisms on a massive scale; a sewage discharge is a significant cause of this undesirable cycle.

Evaporation   The emission of water vapour by a free surface of liquid water at a temperature below boiling point.

Evapotranspiration   The total amount of moisture which evaporates from any specific area of soil and vegetation in a particular ecosystem *q.v.*; being the difference between the total precipitation falling on the area and the amount which runs off as estimated by stream flow, assuming a constant soil-water content.

Exposure   The amount of a particular physical or chemical agent that reaches a receptor *q.v.* or target.

External Effects   or externalities. Social costs and benefits caused by the activities of an industry which are not reflected in the price at which the product is sold, or influence the quantities purchased; costs not borne by those who occasion them, and benefits not paid for by the recipients. In the generation and supply of electricity, two externalities are:

1. those costs to the community of grit emission from old power stations
2. those benefits to the community of replacing dirty fuels with clean electricity, thus reducing air pollution in cities at the point of use.

The cost or benefit is external to the industry and does not find its way into the price charged the ultimate consumer; thus the electrical energy market, among others, is imperfect in giving the consumer incorrect information about the cost of resources used to produce power. The economist, R. Turvey, has suggested that externalities should be "internalized", if they are known to have a significant effect on the demand or cost structure of a product, i.e. corrections should be made to allow for them when calculating marginal cost. Marginal cost thus becomes a social opportunity cost, or true cost.

F

Family   In relation to taxonomy *q.v.*, a commonly utilized category of classification that incorporates a range of genera possessing a number of characteristics in common.

Fanning   Descriptive of the behaviour of a chimney plume when the air is very stable, the gases quickly reaching their equilibrium level and travelling horizontally with sideways meanderings but with very little dilution and mixing in the vertical direction. Fanning produces a thin but concentrated layer of pollution that may impinge on hillsides or tall buildings.

Fauna The animal life of a geological period or of a region; corresponds to the term flora *q.v.* for plant life. Dr. H. J. Frith has indicated that present-day fauna in Australia includes over 60,000 species of insects, some 130 species of amphibians, about 400 species of reptiles, about 230 species of mammals, and over 700 species of birds.

Feral Descriptive of animals or plants that are no longer domesticated or cultivated and have reverted to a wild state.

Fertilizers Materials which, when added to soil, stimulate the growth of crops. Animal manures and vegetational wastes have been applied for thousands of years; natural organic fertilizers applied today include manure, compost, and sawdust, while inorganic fertilizers include crushed limestone, gypsum, sulphur, and rock phosphate. In addition, vast amounts of manufactured chemical compounds of nitrogen, potassium, phosphorus, and sulphur are applied. Many of these manufactured fertilizers are quite soluble, and if not taken up by plants are easily leached away; their movement out of the soil by run-off *q.v.* or by drainage may have a significant impact on water quality. Thus appreciable quantities of nitrates may be leached to water. Nitrate fertilizers may also pose a health hazard if excessive nitrites occur in food, particularly leafy vegetables, and in drinking water.

See also Eutrophication, Green Revolution, Methaemoglobinaemia, Nutrient Stripping.

Fibrosa Obliterans Formation of fibrous tissue.

Flood Plain A relatively smooth portion of a river valley, adjacent to the river channel, built of sediments carried by the river and which is covered with water when the river overflows its banks. An example, is the Serpentine area at the mouth of the Brisbane River; because of the potentially hazardous effects of filling on the Brisbane River flood plain, the desirability of using this low-lying area for refuse disposal has now been questioned.

Flora   The plant life of a geological period or of a region; corresponds to the term fauna *q.v.* for animal life.

Fluoridation   The addition of fluoride to public water supplies in appropriate cases as an additional precaution against dental decay. Water containing the optimal amount of fluoride appears to increase resistance to tooth decay, while waters containing too much fluoride are capable of producing dental fluorosis, a mottling of the tooth enamel associated with brittleness and general deterioration.

Fluoride occurs naturally in water and, in some cases, in adequate amounts. In a cool climate, any potable water supply containing less than 0.8 gram per cubic metre of fluoride is considered deficient; the optimal quantity usually recommended is 1.0 gram per cubic metre (equivalent to 1.0 milligram per litre, or 1 part per million parts, by weight). In warmer climates, such as Australia, a smaller amount may be satisfactory. The World Health Organization regards fluoridation as a landmark in the history of public health. Investigation appears to affirm that wherever fluoridation has been introduced, dental decay in the teeth of children has been reduced by 65 to 75 per cent. It is claimed that this has been demonstrated in the United Kingdom, the United States of America, Canada, Western Germany, the Soviet Union, and in various parts of Australia.

Fluorides   Compounds containing fluorine, the lightest and most reactive of the halogens. Fluorides occur widely in rocks and soils; consequently, gaseous and particulate fluorides are emitted from many industrial operations using natural materials, e.g.

1. electrolysis of cryolite during the manufacture of aluminium
2. use of fluorspar as a flux in the steel industry
3. sintering of phosphate rock
4. superphosphate manufacture
5. thermal processing of electric furnace slag
6. cement manufacture
7. from brick and pottery kilns.

Peach, tomato, corn and bean crops have been severely injured by short exposures to very low concentrations of hydrogen fluoride. In semi-rural Florida, east of Tampa, large amounts of fluorides emitted from phosphate plants have been deposited on nearby citrus groves, ranches and gladiolus farms; orange and lemon trees have produced smaller yields, and gladioli have turned brown and died. Fluorosis in cattle has occurred in the United Kingdom; lameness in affected animals was the chief source of loss although there was also a loss in milk yield. Sources of fluorides have included basic open hearth steel works, potteries, tileworks, brickworks, vitreous enamel works, and combustion gases from large plants burning low grade coal.

Fly Ash   Low density, finely divided material carried over in the exhaust gases from the incineration of combustible matter.

Fog   Visible moisture in the atmosphere *q.v.* By international agreement, fog is defined as visibility below 1,000 metres. In general it does not become a major hindrance or nuisance to the public until the visibility falls below 200 metres. The atmosphere always contains water vapour in varying amounts. If it is cooled in some way below a certain temperature, called the dew-point temperature, condensation will take place and small droplets of water will be formed. These droplets may form as a suspension around the very small particles which are always present in the air or they may form directly on to the cooling surfaces as dew drops. Hence, before fog can form, the air must be cooled below a certain temperature. The mechanisms for cooling the air are as follows:

1. Radiation — On a clear night the earth's surface radiates heat to space and receives little or none in return. It cools. The air adjacent to the ground is cooled by conduction and continues to cool at a greater rate than the layers of air above. After a time the surface air is cooled below the dew-point temperature and fog is formed. The fog layer will thicken as the cooling process continues and eventually may have a depth of a few metres or several scores of metres.

2. Advection — At times a slow change in the overall weather pattern gives rise to the slow movement of moist warm air over a cold surface (e.g. a snow surface). The result is that the surface layers are again cooled

below the dew-point temperature and fog is formed. It should be stressed that for both mechanisms to operate, the wind must be very light or calm.

Food Chain   A chain of organisms through which energy is transferred; each link in the chain feeds on and obtains energy from the one preceding it and, in turn, is eaten by and provides energy for, the one following it. An ecosystem *q.v.* consists of numerous food chains, although the two major categories of food chain are the grazing food chain and the detritus food chain.

Food Web   An interconnected series of food chains.

Foraminifera   Unicellular marine animals mostly of microscopic size with shells of various composition.

Free Acceleration Test   The most popular method for the road-side testing of commercial vehicles. The engine is rapidly accelerated in neutral gear, the smoke emitted being measured directly and continuously by an approved smoke meter. The maximum smoke density is taken as an indication of smoke density likely to be emitted on the road. Several countries have adopted this test as the basis of their legislation. The introduction of such a technique for the first time obviously involves establishing a satisfactory correlation between the results of the free acceleration test and observed smoke emissions under actual operating conditions. In addition to this road-side test, it might well become desirable for all diesel trucks to undergo an annual engine and chassis dynamometer test at an approved testing station, as part of an annual vehicle check for licence renewal purposes.

Front   A relatively narrow zone of transition between air masses. If a cold air mass is displacing a warm one, the transition is called a cold front, and vice versa. Fronts are associated usually with low pressure areas and pressure troughs.

Fuel Efficiency   The proportion of the potential heat of a fuel which is converted into a useful form of energy.

Fuel Element   A unit in the core of a nuclear reactor *q.v.* which contains the fissile material used as fuel.

Fulham-Simon-Carves Process   A process for removing sulphur dioxide *q.v.* from flue gases using ammonia liquor as the washing medium. The process consists essentially in scrubbing the gases with ammonia liquor to produce ammonium salts which, by autoclaving, are converted into ammonium sulphate and sulphur. The advantage of the process is that it produces saleable products.

See Battersea Gas Washing Process.

Fume   Airborne solid particles arising from the condensation of vapours or from chemical reactions; fume particles are generally less than 5 μ in size, respirable, and visible as a cloud. They may be emitted in the following processes:

1. volatilization
2. sublimation
3. distillation
4. calcination
5. chemical reaction.

Fumigation   A rapid increase in air pollution at ground level caused by turbulence of the atmosphere created by a rising morning sun following a nocturnal inversion in which pollutants have become concentrated aloft; very high ground-level concentrations may be experienced for an hour or more, sometimes at a distance of many kilometres from the source of the pollution. This fumigation effect

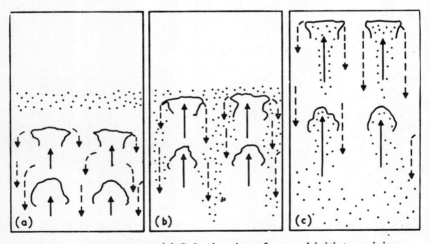

Figure 3   Fumigation: (a) Solar heating of ground initiates mixing by up-currents; (b) Fumigation occurs as mixing involves layer of polluted air; (c) Dilution, as clean air is introduced from above (Source: Warren Spring Laboratory, Stevenage, England)

during the break-up of an inversion is due to the restoration of turbulence initially at ground level which gradually penetrates into the stable layers above which are still acting as a "lid" inhibiting the upward dispersal of pollutants. Fumigation was originally described by E. W. Hewson in an article "The meteorological control of atmospheric pollution by heavy industry", Quarterly Journal Royal Meteorological Society 71, (1945) 266–282.

See Figure 3.

G

Gamma Radiation   Electromagnetic radiation of very short wavelength, consisting of high-energy photons. Their penetrating power is much greater than that of alpha and beta rays, but their ionizing power is much lower.

See Alpha Radiation, Beta Radiation.

Garbage   Animal, fruit, or vegetable residues resulting from the handling, preparation, and cooking of foods.

Genome   The total gene complement of an individual organism.

Genotype   The genetic constitution or inherited properties possessed by an organism, as contrasted with the characteristics displayed by the organism.

See Phenotype.

Genus   A taxonomic category which represents a hypothetical assemblage of species populations having a number of characteristics in common.

Geological Time Scale   The time scale for the different eras and periods which comprise the history of the earth.

See Table 2.

Geomorphology   The study of the form and development of the earth, especially its surface and physical features, and the relationship between these features and the geological structures underneath.

Geosphere   The solid, non-living portion of the earth; a concept which excludes the atmosphere, hydrosphere, and biosphere *qq.v.*

Geostrophic Wind   A horizontal equilibrium wind, blowing parallel to the isobars, which represents an exact balance

Era	Period	Epoch	Age in Years
Cenozoic (recent life)	Quaternary	Recent	10,000
		Pleistocene	2,000,000
	Tertiary	Pliocene	7,000,000
		Miocene	25,000,000
		Oligocene	40,000,000
		Eocene	60,000,000
		Paleocene	70,000,000
Mesozoic (intermediate life)	Cretaceous		135,000,000
	Jurassic		180,000,000
	Triassic		225,000,000
Palaeozoic (ancient life)	Permian		270,000,000
	Carboniferous		350,000,000
	Devonian		400,000,000
	Silurian		440,000,000
	Ordovician		500,000,000
	Cambrian		600,000,000
Precambrian			3,500,000,000

Table 2   Geological time scale

between the horizontal pressure-gradient force and the horizontal component of the coriolis *q.v.* or inertia force.

Geosynclinal Belts   Large, elongated zones of the earth's crust which have experienced a complex history of subsidence, sediment-infilling, volcanic activity and deformation. With few exceptions, the major mountain systems of the world have formed on such belts, e.g., the Alps, Andes, Himalayas and Rockies.

Geothermal   Pertaining to the heat of the interior of the earth. This heat may be sometimes harnessed, through the medium of hot water and steam, for heating and other purposes; this is done in the Rotorua area of New Zealand. *See* Figure 4.

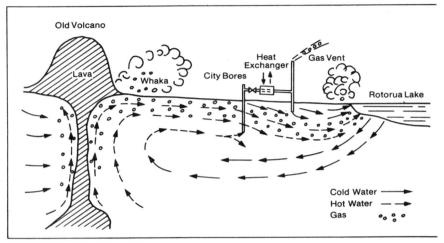

Figure 4 City bores, Rotorua, New Zealand (Source: Department of Health, New Zealand)

Grab Sample A sample of gas or liquid taken over a very short period of time, a time insignificant compared with the total duration of the operation.

Great Barrier Reef An extensive area of continental shelf comprising the calcareous skeletal remains of coral, algae, molluscs, sea urchins and other forms of life which extends from Gladstone on the Queensland coast, north to the Torres Strait. An outstanding area of live coral and associated fauna, the reef is nearly 2,400 kilometres in length, with a width varying from about 30 kilometres to 300 kilometres. Parts of the reef are exposed at low tide, but otherwise it lies beneath a shallow sea. The oil industry has sought permission to drill through the reef to ascertain the existence of oil thought to exist in sedimentary rock lying beneath the reef. The question of drilling and its associated hazards has been the subject of investigation by a Royal Commission.

See also Crown-of-Thorns Starfish.

Green Bans Work bans on projects considered by the participants to be likely to impair the general environment.

Notably, many green bans have been imposed by the Builders Labourers' Federation in Sydney halting construction of buildings, freeways through the inner city, and carparks, and saving parkland. They were imposed only after the union had been approached by residents, conservationists, or architets. Green bans stand in contrast to black bans which unions traditionally impose in an attempt to compel employers or governments to improve wages and working conditions; green bans are imposed to preserve living conditions. Several unions participated in bans on the construction of Newport 'D' power station in Melbourne on environmental grounds. Such bans are feasible and effective, as long as the work force can afford to forgo the earnings that such projects provide.

Green Belts   Belts of land of irregular shape, usually several kilometres wide, around urban areas. Their purpose is to prevent further expansion; prevent the coalescence of neighbouring conurbations; and perhaps to channel the growth of a conurbation in a certain direction or to preserve the special character of some historic cities. The London Green Belt was approved in 1959. One notable example has been the reduction of the natural dust hazards at Broken Hill by the creation of a green belt surrounding the city. Once livestock were prevented from grazing on the area set aside for regeneration, nature re-asserted herself and today the duststorms which were a feature of pre-war Broken Hill are now intermittent events. This project was started long before conservation and the environment were receiving today's prominence.

Greenhouse Effect   The property of selective absorption used in the construction of greenhouses which finds a parallel in the general atmosphere *q.v.* Water vapour and carbon dioxide *q.v.,* although only a minute fraction of the mass of the atmosphere, exercise considerable influence over the heat balance of the atmosphere and ground. While relatively transparent to incoming shortwave solar radiation they are relatively opaque to long wave back-radiation from the earth, hence they exercise a warming or greenhouse effect. A secular increase in carbon dioxide in the atmosphere, arising from progressive industrialization and the combustion of fossil fuels, could raise the mean temperature of the atmosphere, effecting profound climatic changes. On the other hand, an increase in aerosols in the atmosphere, also due to industrial emissions, could cool the earth through a reflection of solar radiation. The arguments concerning the actual trends and effects in the atmosphere are presently inconclusive, but this aspect of the effects of consuming fossil fuels merits the closest study.

Green Manuring The process of turning under green crops to improve soil productivity; its effects on soil are similar to those of animal manure.

Green Revolution The establishment of new crop records through the adoption of new varieties of wheat and rice, associated often with heavy inputs of fertilizers and improved irrigation. Closely associated with the name of Norman E. Borlaug, a U.S. agronomist, who successfully developed strains of grain that increased yields in several countries dramatically. The benefits have been felt in the Middle East, the Far East, North Africa and Latin America. Wheat production in Mexico multiplied sixfold during the quarter-century Borlaug worked with the Mexican government; 'dwarf' wheat imported in the mid-1960s was responsible for a 60 per cent increase in Pakistan and India. Borlaug was the winner of the 1970 Nobel Peace Prize.

Green Stamp Plan A proposal by Professor Kenneth E. Boulding to provide a market mechanism for population control. According to the plan, each human being would receive in adolescence, say, 110 green stamps, 100 of which would enable the owner to have one legal child. A market would then be set up in these instruments so that those who had a strong desire for children could buy stamps from those who did not want to have children. Individual preferences in this matter could thus be expressed while at the same time society could maintain overall social control of the rate of growth of population. There would presumably have to be mild sanctions, argues Professor Boulding, for having illegal children which might entail temporary sterilization until the illegal children are paid for in green stamps. Professor Boulding has remarked (not surprisingly) that his scheme has met with a good deal of disapproval.

Grit and Dust   Solid particle pollution, the source of many complaints by residents and industry. Dusts are solid particles produced in the course of combustion and processes such as crushing, grinding and demolition. Particles may be as small as 1 μm in size; particles larger than about 76 μm in size are generally referred to as grit. Only particles which are smaller than about 5 μm insize are capable of penetrating to the alveoli, or air sacs, of the lungs. This division between respirable and non-respirable ranges (at a particle diameter of about 5 μm) is today widely recognised and forms the basis of mining regulations in Britain.

The extent to which particles are retained in the lungs is partly dependent on their size. Dr. P. J. Lawther of the British Medical Research Council has stated that the maximum retention in the alveoli is thought to occur when the inhaled particles are about 1.5 μm in diameter. The percentage retention falls as the particle size approaches 0.3 μm; cigarette smoke comprises particles of about this size.

Considering the wide range of processes which emit dust, clearly the composition of dust may vary just as widely. The commonest dust emitted from chimneys is, however, fly ash. Fly ash is simply fine ash released during the combustion of coal and carried through the boiler or furnace flue system by the draught. Ash not deposited in the flues or arrested in dust collectors is discharged to atmosphere.

Dr. S. R. Craxford, formerly of the Warren Spring Laboratory, Stevenage, England, has expressed the opinion that the average urban grit and dust fall in Britain of 113 mg/m^2/d (8.7 tons/mile^2/month) passes, if not unnoticed, as at least acceptable as a minor drawback of town life. When the figure much exceeds 200 mg/m^2/d (15.4 tons/mile^2/month) the inhabitants begin to realize that they are living in an unpleasantly dusty locality. Figures of about 300 mg/m^2/d (23.0 tons/mile^2/month) and above indicate gross pollution.

In Western Australia, at Port Hedland, the ore-handling facilities originally created a dust nuisance in the township. In the planning of the ore-handling facilities, dust extractors were designed for all parts of the plant, but extraction efficiency was found to be insufficient. Subsequently a pressure-atomized spray system was installed to feed moisture in at many different points, bringing total expenditure on dust control at the port to in excess of $1 million.

Gross Domestic Product at Constant Prices The Gross National Domestic Product (at either factor cost or market prices) taken over a series of years and adjusted to discount changes in the value of money, thus giving a measure of the real change in national income over the period. The trend in the Gross Domestic Product at constant prices is not, however, a comprehensive measure of changes in the national well-being, or in the progress towards an improvement in the 'quality of life' *q.v.* For example, things tangible and intangible that cannot be purchased in the market place are excluded from the statistical measurement of Gross Domestic Product; public expenditure to relieve traffic congestion and added to the real leisure time of commuters adds nothing, on that score, to the G.D.P. Expenditure on cars causes the G.D.P. to apparently grow faster than if the same amounts were devoted to education, health, and culture. The problem is to maximize the real welfare of the community, not simply a statistical measure of growth.

Gross Domestic Product at Factor Cost The value of goods and services produced within the nation, representing only the sum of the incomes of the factors of production. It is equal to the Gross Domestic Product at market prices *q.v.*, minus indirect taxes plus subsidies. Valuation at factor cost displays the composition of the Gross Domestic Product in terms of the factors of production employed, the contributions of the factors being measured by the incomes they receive as wages, salaries, profits, interest, and rent.

Gross Domestic Product at Market Prices The value of goods and services produced within the nation, charged at ruling prices. Prices include all taxes on expenditure, subsidies being regarded as negative taxes.

Gross Productivity The rate at which energy is procured by a particular trophic level *q.v.* or levels in an ecosystem *q.v.*

i.e. the rate at which energy is "fixed" by plants through photosynthesis *q.v.* Plants use a considerable portion of the energy they fix for the purposes of respiration; gross productivity minus this respiration rate is known as "net productivity". Net productivity appears as plant tissue or biomass *q.v.* Biomass present in a given area or volume at a given time is the "standing crop".

Ground-water Water which occupies the pores and crevices of rock and soil, as opposed to surface-water *q.v.* which runs off into streams. Ground-water is particularly vulnerable to pollution because of its low self-cleansing capacity.
    See Aquifer, Water-Table.

Groyne A shore-protection structure extended into the sea at an angle to trap sand and reduce erosion by currents, tides, and waves.
    See Coastal Protection.

Gully Reclamation Techniques for checking erosion; small gullies may be ploughed in and suitably seeded, or check dams may be constructed along a gully allowing silt collecting behind the dams to gradually fill in the channel. In appropriate cases, the soil may be stabilized by planting rapid-growing shrubs and trees.
    See Soil Erosion

Gustiness A form of turbulence *q.v.* set up near the ground by obstacles presented to the direct flow of air, e.g. buildings and surface irregularities.

H

Habitat A physical portion of the environment *q.v.* that is inhabited by an organism or population *q.v.* of organisms. A habitat is characterized by a relative uniformity of the physical environment and fairly close interaction of all the biological species involved. In terms of regions, a habitat may comprise a desert, a tropical forest, a prairie field, the Arctic Tundra or the Arctic Ocean.

Haemoglobin (Hb) A respiratory pigment found in the blood plasma, it combines readily with oxygen to form oxyhaemoglobin and has a still greater affinity for carbon monoxide.

See Carboxyhaemoglobin.

Half-Life   The time taken for one-half of the atoms of a radioactive isotope to disintegrate. Each isotope has a unique half-life. Iodine 131 has a half-life of 8 days; strontium 90 a half-life of about 28 years; caesium 137 a half-life of about 30 years; and radium a half-life of 1,580 years.

Halocline   The boundary between two masses of water, e.g. the surface waters of the Baltic which have a lower salinity *q.v.*, due to the contribution of the fresher waters of the rivers, than the corresponding current carrying the inflow of more saline water at a greater depth. Seen generally, the boundary between these masses — the halocline — is at a depth of about 60 metres. The layering is essentially stable since the bottom water, being more saline, is denser.

Halophyte   A plant that tolerates a very salty soil.

Hardness   A characteristic of water representing the total concentration of calcium and magnesium ions. Hardness is expressed fundamentally in terms of the chemical equivalents of metal ions capable of precipitating soap; it is also expressed in terms of the equivalent amount of calcium carbonate. Hard water requires a good deal more soap than soft water to make a good lather. Where hardness is due mainly to the presence of bicarbonates of calcium and magnesium it is described as "temporary"; if due to the sulphates and chlorides of calcium and magnesium it is described as "permanent". However, both kinds of hardness may be reduced substantially by the use of appropriate techniques, e.g. the lime-soda process followed, if necessary, by the ion-exchange process. Hard water is considered unsuitable for some industrial processes as it leaves scaly deposits in pipes and steam generators; pre-treatment is essential. On the other hand, for irrigation purposes a hard water is preferred for it reacts more favourably with soils and readily reaches the root zone.

Hazardous Wastes   Wastes containing any substance which may present danger:

1. to the life or health of living organisms when released

into the environment

2. to the safety of humans or equipment in disposal plants if incorrectly handled.

Hazardous wastes have been further classified to define the particular hazard as follows:

1. Toxic, e.g. most pesticides, lead salts, arsenic compounds, cadmium compounds, cattle dips
2. Flammable, e.g. hydrocarbons
3. Corrosive e.g. acids or alkalies
4. Oxidizing e.g. nitrates or chromates.

Some substances may be hazardous on more than one count. The uncontrolled disposal of hazardous wastes has resulted in contamination of surface streams and underground waters to an extent that the waters are dangerous to plant and animal life. The underground waters in the aquifers of Victoria are already of importance in many uses and may be of much greater importance in the future; once polluted these underground waters remain polluted and unuseable for many years.

See Aquifer, Surface-Water, Underground Water, Waste.

Health   Defined in the preamble to the constitution of the World Health Organisation as " . . . a state of complete physical, mental and social well-being and not merely the absence of disease or infirmity." This definition has been widely accepted in broad principle; however, suitable techniques for measuring health, as so defined, have not evolved and most assessments of health effects rely upon mortality and morbidity *qq.v.* statistics.

Hectare   A metric unit of area equal to 10,000 square metres, or 2.471 acres.

Heptachlor   A solid insecticide, $C_{10}H_5Cl_7$, belonging to the chlorinated hydrocarbon group; similar to chlordane.

Herbicide   An agent, frequently a chemical, used to kill plants.

Herbivore   A heterotrophic *q.v.* organism which obtains energy from the consumption of plants.

See Carnivore, Omnivore.

Heterotrophic   Descriptive of organisms which obtain energy from the break-down of complex organic substances. All animals and fungi are heterotrophic.

Hexachlorobenzene (HCB)   A fungicide for seed grain and vegetable seeds, it is a by-product from the production of chlorine gas and chlorinated hydrocarbons. Residue levels have been found in the fatty tissues of cattle and sheep at the time of slaughter for human consumption.

High Level Inversion On occasions an inversion *q.v.* of temperature is formed well above the earth's surface (i.e. upwards of 300 metres or more). This acts as a lid, preventing the ascent of chimney plumes. It is formed by the slow descent of air which becomes warmer by adiabatic *q.v.* compression since the descent is inevitably into a level of higher pressure. This is known as a "subsidence inversion". It is associated with anticyclones in which air descends at a rate of perhaps 1,000 metres per day. Cloud may form under such an inversion and will be carried inland by the wind. If the wind speed is sufficiently large the cloud and the inversion will be maintained and the sun will be unable to 'burn' the cloud away. Effluent will be trapped under such an inversion, but the existence of the cloud pre-supposes air movement. If the wind drops, the cloud disperses and the inversion also. However, thermal convection may bring some of the accumulated pollution to ground level, by way of fumigation *q.v.*

Holarctic The biogeographical region *q.v.* that includes the Nearctic (or temperate and arctic North America and Greenland) and the Palaearctic (or Europe, the northern parts of Africa, the Arabian Peninsula, and Asia north of the Himalayas).

Holocene The later of the two geologic epochs comprising the Quaternary period; i.e., the time period from the close of the Pleistocene or Glacial epoch (about 10,000 years ago) through the present; synonymous with Recent. *See* Geological Time Scale.

Homeostasis A feedback mechanism which effects a balanced condition in a biological process. A stable system is one that responds to changes from a steady state by developing forces to restore it to the original condition, for example, the density dependent *q.v.* regulation of population *q.v.* implies a homeostatic mechanism. As a population increases and approaches the point when the energy base, or the physical limitations on nesting sites and shelter, will support few more, population growth slows and the absolute population may decline; however when a population declines significantly below a level which the habitat can support, the birth rate increases, the death rate declines, and the population expands again. Thus homeostatic processes account in part for long-term fluctuations in animal populations; population fluctuations may be also environmentally induced, e.g. through the influence of weather and climate.

Homeothermous In living organisms, the maintenance of a steady body temperature particularly through the operation of internal physiological mechanisms.

Home Range The area over which an animal moves in seeking and obtaining its food.

Human Progress Index A proposed index of gross national welfare, or total human progress as opposed to purely economic progress. The need for such an index has arisen from widespread discontent with the use of the concepts of the Gross Domestic Product (or the Gross National Product) as the measure of human progress. An integrated human progress index would reflect a set of social and environmental indices, as well as economic indices. The index would be influenced by such factors as the depletion of non-renewable resources; trends in air and water pollution; the effects of developments on noise levels; hours of work and travel time; access to cultural and recreational activities; the depressing effects of heavy unemployment; and the range of educational opportunities open to the child.

Humate A salt or ester of a humic acid, derived from humus *q.v.* during the decomposition of organic matter in soils.

Humification The microbial breakdown of dead organic matter in the soil to form the largely inert product humus *q.v.*

Humus A complex organic component of the soil, resulting from the decomposition of plant and animal tissue; it gives soil *q.v.* its characteristically dark colour and is of great importance for plant growth. The term is also used for a dark brown or almost black complex organic material residue left after the completion of biochemical processes in sewage treatment *q.v.* works.

Hydrocarbons Organic compounds consisting of carbon and hydrogen only. They are subdivided into aliphatic and cyclic hydrocarbons according to the arrangement of the carbon atoms in the molecule. The aliphatic hydrocarbons are in turn subdivided into:
1. paraffins
2. olefins
3. diolefins, etc., according to the number of double bonds in the molecule.

The cyclic hydrocarbons are subdivided into:
1. aromatics
2. naphthemes or cyclo-paraffins.

In all types of hydrocarbons, hydrogen atoms may be replaced by other atoms making the formation of a virtually endless number of compounds possible. Hydrocarbons are found commonly in fossil fuels and in the products of the partial combustion of these substances, e.g. in the exhaust gases of petrol-driven vehicles.

Hydrogen Sulphide A colourless gas with a density greater than air and a characteristic foul odour of rotten eggs. It arises in the decomposition of organic material. Other sources include oil refineries, sulphur recovery plants, some metallurgical processes, and various chemical industries using sulphur-containing compounds. Hydrogen sulphide is the principal air pollution problem in New Zealand both from indigenous sources and from organic wastes associated with the primary industries (timber pulping, meat packaging, skin curing, etc.). It is emitted from the ground in the Rotorua area of the North Island and is present in the mineral waters of that area. Hydrogen sulphide is irritating to the eyes and respiratory tract; it leads to death through paralysis of the respiratory centre of the brain. Though the odour of hydrogen sulphide is readily recognizable in low concentrations, the detection of dangerous concentrations by smell is unreliable and unsafe as olfactory fatigue occurs quickly at high concentrations. The gas is corrosive to many metals and even when present in the atmosphere in concentrations below the level of physiological significance it discolours lead paints. Hydrogen sulphide tends to be a localized problem; in ordinary combustion processes the gas is readily burned to sulphur dioxide *q.v.*

Hydrograph   A graph indicating the level of water, e.g. in a watercourse or well; or the rate of flow of water through time.

Hydrological Cycle   The continual exchange of water between the earth and the atmosphere *q.v.* Since the height of the ocean surfaces remains essentially unchanged from year to year, evaporation from the oceans must equal the rainfall over the oceans plus the run-off from rivers and streams and effluent discharges.

See Figure 5.

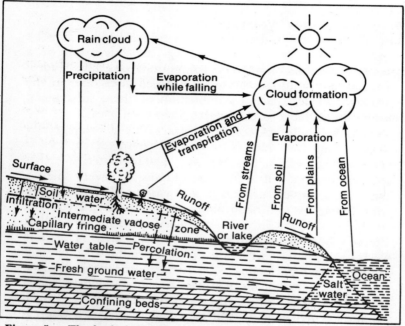

Figure 5   The hydrological cycle (Source: Report of the Australian Senate Select Committee on *Water Pollution*, Canberra: Australian Government Printer, 1970)

Hydroponics   or nutriculture. The technique of growing crops in an aqueous nutrient solution, without soil.

Hydrosphere   That part of the earth comprising water, e.g. oceans, lakes and rivers.

Hydrostatic Pressure   The pressure exerted by water at rest, at any point within the water body; as, in the case of ground-water *q.v.*, the pressure caused by the weight of water in the same zone of saturation above a given point.

Hygroscopic   Readily attracting or absorbing moisture from the atmosphere *q.v.*

Hyperkinesis   Excessive motility (activity or movement) of a person, or of muscles.

Hypolimnion   The bottom stratum of water in a lake, below the thermocline *q.v.*, which, like the epilimnion *q.v.*, shows a temperature gradient of less than one degree C per metre of depth.

I

Igneous Rock   Rock formed by solidification from a molten or partially molten state. Contrasted with sedimentary rock *q.v.*

Imhoff Tank   A primary sewage treatment *q.v.* process combining sedimentation with anaerobic *q.v.* sludge digestion in one tank; there is no mechanical equipment. The sewage flows through the upper or sedimentation chamber, the deposited sludge passing through slots into a digestion chamber below. The sludge removal is thus automatic, these tanks having certain advantages over separate sedimentation and sludge digestion tanks. Imhoff tanks are used extensively in Australia.

Incineration   A method of treating refuse *q.v.* to reduce the volume and weight and to leave an innocuous residue.

The early type of incinceration plants were known as destructors, and often of the batch-type as against the now normally-used continuous-feed plants. A modern incineration plant is usually constructed where land-fill *q.v.* disposal sites are distant from the centre of generation of refuse, making transfer and transportation of refuse a costly proposition.

Incipient Lethal Level   That level of a toxic substance beyond which 50 per cent of a population *q.v.* of organisms cannot live for an indefinite period of time. Incipient lethal levels denote threshold concentrations.

See Application Fator.

Indicator Species   Those species *q.v.* in a habitat *q.v.* which are most sensitive to slight changes in environmental factors. When determined, their decline can serve as an early warning of the endangerment of the health *q.v.* of the community *q.v.*

Indigenous Native or original to an area; not introduced from outside the particular region or environment *q.v.*

Industrial Effluent The water- and air-borne wastes of industry.

Industrialization A process of production characterized by an increasing capital intensity, i.e. by forms of production in which there is an increased use of capital equipment per person employed; by an extensive division of labour; increasingly complex industrial organization; and increasing interdependence between persons and groups.

Infiltration Term commonly applied to the unintended ingress of ground-water *q.v.* into a drainage system.

Interfluve The area of land between adjacent streams.

International Convention for the Prevention of Pollution from Ships A convention concluded in London in November 1973, at the end of the International Marine Pollution Conference, convened by the Intergovernmental Maritime Consultative Organisation (IMCO). The conference — the largest ever held on the subject — was attended by 500 representatives of the leading maritime nations.

The new convention will enter into force twelve months after it has been ratified by 15 countries constituting at least 50 per cent of the world's merchant shipping. When it does enter into force, the 1973 convention will supersede the International Convention for the Prevention of the Pollution of the Sea by Oil 1954 which, however, will remain in force meantime. The 1973 convention forms part of the body of maritime law.

The new instrument contains provisions aimed at eliminating pollution of the sea by both oil and the noxious substances which may be discharged operationally, and at minimizing the amount of oil which would be accidentally released in such mishaps as collisions or strandings.

The convention applies to any ship of any type whatsoever, including hydrofoil boats, air-cushion vehicles, submersibles, floating craft and fixed or floating platforms, operating in the marine environment. It covers all aspects of intentional and accidental pollution from ships by oil or noxious substances carried in bulk or in packages, sewage and garbage. But it does not deal with dumping which is covered by the Convention for the Prevention of Marine Pollution by Dumping from Ships and Aircraft signed in Oslo in 1972 nor the release of harmful substances directly arising from the exploration, exploitation and associated offshore processing of sea-bed mineral resources.

International Referral System   A programme for the international exchange of information on environmental problems and solutions; part of the Action Plan adopted by the United Nations Conference on the Human Environment, 1972 *q.v.*

International Whaling Convention   An International Convention signed in 1946 by representatives from 14 countries. Under the Convention the International Whaling Commission was established for the purpose of safeguarding for future generations 'the great natural resources represented by the whale stocks' and 'to protect all species of whales from further over-fishing'. Member countries may opt out of restrictions, however, if they do not wish to be hampered by them. The Commission has failed to establish any arrangement for the universal policing of factory ships and land stations by neutral observers to ensure that only mature whales of permitted species are taken. Catch quotas well above those giving a sustainable yield have been regularly set. Consequently, several species have been hunted to the point of commercial extinction — notably the Blue, Humpback, and Fin whales. The United Nations Conference on the Human Environment which met in Stockholm in 1972, recommended "that Governments agree to strengthen the International Whaling Commission" and as a matter of urgency "call for an international agreement, under the auspices of the International Whaling Commission and involving all Governments concerned, for a 10-year moratorium on commercial whaling". This proposal failed, but in 1974 the Commission adopted instead an Australian proposal which places an automatic ban on hunting those whale species whose numbers fall below certain levels.

See also Commons.

Inversion   A temperature inversion in the atmosphere *q.v.* in which the temperature, instead of falling, increases with height above the ground. With the colder and heavier air below, there is no tendency to form upward currents and turbulence is suppressed. Inversions are often formed in the late afternoon when the radiation emitted from the ground exceeds that received from the sinking sun. Inversions are also caused by katabatic winds, i.e. cold winds flowing down the hillside into a valley, and by anti-cyclones. In inversion layers, both vertical and horizontal diffusion is inhibited and pollutants become trapped, sometimes for long periods. Low-level discharges of pollutants are more readily trapped by inversions than high-level discharges; furthermore, high-level discharges into an inversion tend to remain at a high level because of the absence of vertical mixing.

See Figure 6.

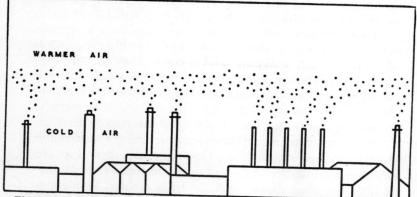

Figure 6   Temperature inversion. A pall of pollution trapped within a stable layer (Source: Warren Spring Laboratory, Stevenage, England)

Ion   An electrically-charged atom.

Ionization   The process by which a neutral atom or group of atoms becomes electrically charged through the loss or gain of electrons.

Ionosphere   A layer of the atmosphere *q.v.* which extends upwards from about 80 kilometres above the surface of the earth. At these levels some of the sun's ultra-violet radiation is absorbed by oxygen and nitrogen molecules which decompose into either free atoms or ionized molecules and atoms.

Irradiation Exposure to rays, e.g. X-rays and ultra-violet rays.

Isohaline A line drawn on a chart or map of an area, indicating points of equal salinity *q.v.*

Isohyets A line on a map connecting points receiving equal rainfall during a stated period.

Isopleth (or Isarithm) A line on a map connecting points at which given variables have the same num rical value (e.g., topographic contour lines).

K

Karyotype The characteristics of the set of chromosomes (in respect of sizes, shapes and numbers) of a representative somatic cell of a given species or individual.
   See Cytotype.

Katabatic Wind A wind caused by cold air flowing downhill. When a sloping land surface cools by night-time radiation, the cold air in contact with the ground flows downhill and along valley bottoms. Opposite of an anabatic wind.
   See Figure 7.

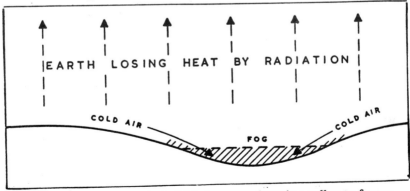

Figure 7 Katabatic wind. Cold air accumulates in a valley to form a persistent temperature inversion (Source: Warren Spring Laboratory, Stevenage, England)

L

Lagoon   An oxidation pond in which waste water is purified through sedimentation, and both aerobic *q.v.* and anaerobic *q.v.* biochemical action over a period of time. Lagoon treatment or "ponding" involves storing liquid waste in natural or artificial lakes, although this storage is provided in different circumstances to achieve different ends. The two main types of lagoon are:

1. Stabilization Lagoon (or Oxidation Pond) A lagoon in which crude sewage or industrial waste is treated. These are used in the southern states of the U.S.A. and in other countries where reasonably long periods of sunshine can be expected throughout the year. Careful maintenance is necessary otherwise this type of lagoon may become a nuisance as a source of odour and mosquito breeding. The technique gives a 60—80 per reduction in biochemical oxygen demand (BOD) and removes 75—85 per cent of the solids. Improvement in performance may be achieved by installing surface aerators.

2. Maturation Lagoon A lagoon or pond for the tertiary treatment of sewage works effluent; a great improvement in the organic quality of an effluent is achieved. A fully oxygenated effluent is produced. A disadvantage of this method of tertiary treatment *q.v.* is the large area occupied by the lagoons.

Laissez-Faire   A policy of non-interference by the State in economic affairs. The underlying philosophy is that man is moved predominantly by self-interest and that there exist certain immutable laws which produce a natural harmony. It is argued that if everyone is left alone to pursue his own interests (to produce, buy and sell, borrow and lend) without outside interference, then the result will be to the mutual benefit of all. The laws of supply and demand will ensure the best deployment of capital and labour; the function of government is, therefore, to act as umpire and not to take part in the game.

Historically, laissez-faire was the expression of the new individualism as applied to industry; it constituted a revolt against all ecclesiastical and governmental interference in the affairs of commerce and industry. Its evolution can be traced back to the fifteenth century. By the early nineteenth century most economists and the governing classes in Britain had come to believe in laissez-faire. The policy found its advocates in Adam Smith (1723—1790), David Ricardo (1772—1823), Thomas Robert Malthus (1776—1834), John Stuart Mill (1806—1873) and John Locke (1632—1704). The practical expression of the philosophy did much to ensure the development of commerce and industry. The system did not produce all the good results that were expected, and the reaction to its failings found expression in factory and health legislation, trade unionism and socialism. In western countries today state intervention in the economic sphere is widespread and increasing; in communist countries it is all embracing. As Sir Hubert Henderson has remarked — "A considerable departure from laissez-faire is necessary in order to realize the theoretical results of laissez-faire!"

Lake Pedder   An isolated lake of unique character, situated in the rugged south-west area of Tasmania. In 1967, the Hydro-Electric Commission of Tasmania submitted to the State Parliament proposals for a hydro-electric scheme on the Gordon River; a necessary consequence of this proposal was the destruction by flooding of Lake Pedder. The Commission recognized that this scheme would result in the loss of the beach at Lake Pedder, but was of the opinion that benefits resulting from the larger lake would outweight this loss. Conservationists have expressed a growing volume of concern regarding the decision on two main grounds:
1. The long-term value for science and the natural attractiveness of the Lake in its original state
2. The commitment of the area to national park purposes in 1955.

Land   One of the factors of production. It is virtually fixed in quantity, although the supply of useful land may be increased by the use of fertilizers, irrigation and machinery, and it can be contracted rapidly on a large scale by neglecting the principles of soil conservation *q.v.* Land, in the economic sense, includes natural resources such as coal, oil and water; natural resources are neither inexhaustible nor rigidly limited. It has no cost of production, and in this respect differs fundamentally from the other two factors, labour and capital.

Land Breeze The movement of air from land to sea. On clear nights the land cools faster than the water, cooling more quickly the lowest layers of air. The heavier land air spills seaward displacing the warmer sea air.

See Sea-Breeze.

Land-Fill The most common form of disposal of refuse *q.v.*; it appears that between 80—90 per cent of the world's refuse will be disposed of by this method for several years to come. The type of sites being used for such disposal are:

1. Mineral excavations
2. Low-lying land
3. Valleys
4. Areas involving the reclamation of land from water
5. Flat land to build up a feature

Generally, in a sanitary land-fill scheme, refuse is tipped in trenches or cells prepared to such a width that the daily input of refuse can be effectively covered, presenting a clean face each day. The refuse can be tipped either at the bottom of the face and dozed into the face, or tipped on top of the previous fill and dozed over the face. It is essential that the refuse be adequately covered and compacted to allow traffic over the fill.

The land-fill method is known in the United Kingdom as "controlled tipping" and in the United States by the fuller title of "sanitary land-fill"; while the content of both expressions is identical, the former emphasises the system by which the waste is deposited while the latter emphasises the hygiene aspects.

Landscape or Amenity Conservation The safeguarding for public enjoyment of scenery or landscape, and of opportunities for outdoor recreation, tourism, field sports, and similar activities; the concept includes the preservation and enhancement not only of what has been inherited but the provision of new amenities and facilities.

Land Use The deployment of land for a variety of uses, e.g. agriculture, industry and commerce, housing, and recreation. Land use planning has as its object the spatial co-ordination of such activities on a national, regional and local level. Through zoning, performance specifications, and building codes, governments can not only specify the uses to which land can be put but also place restrictions on those uses. Controls can prevent the establishment of industries with a high air pollution potential in poorly ventilated basins and valleys; and the establishment of noisy or odorous processes near residential areas.

Lapse Rates The rate of decrease of temperature with increasing height in the atmosphere *q.v.* From the surface to a height of about 11 kilometres, known as the troposphere *q.v.*, the lapse rate is, on average about 6° to 8° C per kilometre. There are considerable departures from this average at all times and at all levels, and it is these departures which characterize the type of weather *q.v.* experienced. If the temperature shows no change with height the condition is described as isothermal. In the stratosphere *q.v.*, the layer of the atmosphere above the troposphere, the lapse rate is isothermal, or very nearly so.

If a parcel of air is displaced upwards without any heat being supplied or removed the air will expand and cool at a rate which is known as the dry adiabatic lapse rate (DALR), the value of which is 10° C per kilometre. This is also known as a "neutral gradient". If a parcel of saturated air is similarly displaced, the cooling will be less than with dry air due to the latent heat made available from the condensation of moisture. The rate at which it cools, known as the saturated adiabatic lapse rate (SALR), is about 6° C per kilometre. The saturated adiabatic lapse rate is not constant at all levels. An atmosphere in which the temperature decreases with height more quickly than the DALR is said to be unstable or superadiabatic. If the lapse rate is negative, i.e. temperature increases with height, the atmosphere is said to be stable; hence the term "temperature inversion", or simply inversion *q.v.* Sometimes the word "stable" is attached to any atmosphere in which the lapse rate is less than the DALR. The actual lapse rate in the atmosphere is known as the environment lapse rate (ELR).

Under average meteorological conditions, the actual temperature gradients lie between 0° and 12° C per kilometre. This variation of +6° to −6° per kilometre from the SALR is known as the "potential temperature gradient".

See Meteorological Influences.

Laterite   A red, highly weathered residual soil *q.v.* characteristic of moist tropical and sub-tropical regions; it is rich in oxides of iron and aluminium .

Leaching   The process by which material such as organic matter and mineral salts is washed out of a layer of soil *q.v.* or dumped material by percolating rain-water; the material washed out is known as leachate.

Leaching Field   A system of open pipes within covered trenches allowing the effluent from a septic tank to enter the surrounding soil.

Lead in Petrol   *See* Tetra Ethyl Lead.

Leukaemia   A frequently fatal disease in which there is an uncontrolled over-production of white blood cells.

Licences   Instruments of control common to much Australian environment legislation, e.g. under the Victorian Environment Protection Act waste discharges from large numbers of installations are controlled through the issue of licences, each licence containing a stringent set of conditions relating to the discharge in terms of volume, nature, and manner of release; licences may be varied or rescinded at any time.

Lidar (Light Detection and Ranging)   A technique used in air pollution *q.v.* research to detect and track chimney plumes at considerable distances, long after they have become invisible to the naked eye.

Lidar was developed for meteorological use in 1963 by M. G. H. Ligda and co-workers at the Stanford Research Institute. The development of the pulsed ruby laser has permitted the direct extension of radar techniques to optical wave lengths. The term "lidar" (light detection and ranging) has come to be applied to such optical radar. Lidar can readily detect the small particles which make up the aerosol content of the atmosphere and smoke plumes.

Lidar equipment comprises:

1. A laser transmitter which emits very brief, high intensity pulses of coherent light.

2. A receiver, which detects the energy at that wavelength backscattered from the atmospheric aerosol as a function of range.

Studies have been undertaken of plume rise from the chimneys of power stations in both the United States and Britain. In Britain much work has been undertaken around Tilbury power station on the River Thames. Initially a searchlight device was employed, but it was found that the searchlight system was insufficiently sensitive in service when used to study plume rise from an oil-fired power station. Subsequently, a lidar device based on a ruby laser was used to measure the highet of the Tilbury plume. This proved a very sensitive device, a response being obtained from all parts of the plume. From a convenient site near Tilbury Power Station observations with the laser were carried out over a considerable range of weather conditions. In conjunction with these measurements twenty-two C.E.R.L. SO_2 measuring instruments were used to determine the corresponding patterns of ground level concentration.

See Figure 8.

Figure 8 A mobile lidar system used by the Central Electricity Research Laboratories in England for research into the dispersion of chimney plumes. Measurements can be made over distances in excess of ten kilometres (Source: Central Office of Information, London)

Life System Concept   That part of an ecosystem *q.v.* which determines the existence, abundance, and evolution of a particular population *q.v.* A life system comprises a subject population and its effective environment *q.v.*; the latter includes all those biotic and abiotic agencies influencing the population. Population and environment are regarded as interdependent elements which function together as a system.

Limnetic Zone   The region of open water beyond the littoral zone *q.v.* of a lake, down to the maximal depth at which there is sufficient sunlight for photosynthesis *q.v.* This is the depth at which photosynthesis balances respiration, known as the compensation depth. Rooted plants are absent in this zone, but there is a great abundance of phytoplankton *q.v.*

Limnology   The scientific study of the physical, chemical, and biological condition of lakes, ponds, and streams.

Lindane   An insecticide and herbicide consisting of a white, water-insoluble powder, $C_6H_6Cl_6$.

Lipid   One of a group of naturally-occurring fats or fatlike materials consisting of the higher fatty acids, their naturally-occurring compounds, and substances found naturally in chemical association with them.

Lithosphere   The earth's crust enclosing the kernel of the earth or barysphere. It is commonly considered as extending to a depth of about eighty kilometres from the surface of the earth; however only the outer part of it or biogeosphere is associated with any form of life..

Littoral   Relating to or taking place on or near the shore.

Littoral Drift   Sand moved under the effect of longshore current; it carries sand which has been stirred into suspension by the turbulence of the breaking waves. The direction and strength of the waves determine the direction and magnitude of the littoral transport at a given time. Determining the direction and average net annual amount of the littoral drift is important in developing shore protection plans. Onshore and offshore sand movements caused by low swells and steep waves respectively, coupled with littoral drift, help to explain the major shoreline changes on the open coasts of the world.

Littoral Zone   The shallow, marginal region of a lake,

characterized by rooted vegetation; the area where sunlight is able to penetrate to the lake bottom, the zone sustaining a high level of photosynthetic activity. A small shallow pond may consist entirely of littoral zone, while a deep lake with an abruptly sloping basin may possess an extremely restricted littoral zone. Per unit volume of water, the littoral zone yields more biomass *q.v.* than either the limnetic or profundal zones *qq.v.*

"Load-On-Top" System A code of practice aimed at minimizing pollution from oil-carrying ships; it involves passing the washings from tank cleaning operations and residue from discharge of the original ballast water to an empty cargo tank nominated as the "slop" tank. Fresh oil cargo is loaded on top of the final residue left after further discharges of water, the resulting mixture being acceptable to refineries despite some additional cost in removing the salt and water. Under the International Convention for the Prevention of Pollution fromShips, 1973 *q.v.*, all oil-carrying ships will be required to be capable of operating with this method of retention, or alternatively to discharge to reception facilities.

Location of Industry, Factors Influencing The factors influencing the location of industry may be defined as:
  1. Availability and cost of raw materials of satisfactory quality and security of future supplies
  2. Delivery costs of sending the final product to markets of sufficient size and certainty, and competitiveness of the product in those markets
  3. Availability of labour having regard both to number and degree of competence required
  4. Transport and communications
  5. Level of local costs generally (rents, rates, wages, etc.)
  6. Adequacy of local resources such as water supply and facilities for waste disposal
  7. Availability, reliability and cost of fuel
  8. Availability of local specialized industries and services
  9. Load-bearing requirements for site
  10. Cost of site development (land cost, levelling, filling, drainage, roads, etc.)
  11. Possibility of development of site for additional plant in due course

12. Availability of housing, local transportation, schools, churches, hospitals and recreation facilities

13. Planning and development restrictions and inducements.

Clearly the "weighting" given to each of these items will vary according to the type of business activities involved. The primary reason for a plant location study by a company is to find a site at which a plant of suitable size can produce the highest return on invested capital; the aim is to establish the optimum location. The problem of location involves highly complex studies concerned not only with present but also future conditions and changing patterns, and often involves difficult decisions.

Planning and industrial development cannot be dissociated from the concept of the socially-responsible utilization (or conservation) of resources, and with larger objectives which may be regarded as desirable by some, such as "zero population growth" or "zero industrial growth" and a stable standard of living. These concepts, accepted as social objectives, would restrict industrial development to industrial change in a qualitative sense associated with only small or zero quantitative expansion. Even well short of these objectives, if a Barrier Reef or Santa Barbara shore is to be preserved unimpaired, then it may be desirable to forgo the potential benefits of oil-drilling in such areas. There is certainly an increasing tendency in public policy towards the exclusion of certain industries from certain areas on the simple proposition that the social penalties would outweight any social gains. The nature of a "social penalty" and a "social gain" is bound to shift with any shift in "social values", but the general thrust today is undoubtedly in the direction of some restraint on unbridled industrial expansion. Industry today is careful to pay lip-service to such ideals, while not always matching promise with performance.

Logistic Curve An S-shaped curve of population growth which is initially slow, then steepens, and finally flattens out at an asymptote determined by the carrying capacity q.v. of the environment q.v.

London Smog Incidents Acute episodes of heavy pollution associated with natural fog covering the Greater London area.

The fog which covered the Greater London area during the four days 5–8 December 1952, was on a much different plane to those previously experienced. An anticyclone *q.v.* reached London from the north-west in the early hours of 5 December and then became stationary. On 6–7 December, London Airport had a minimum air temperature of −5 and −6° C and a maximum just under 0° C. Soundings showed two inversions *q.v.*, one close to the surface and the other caused by descending (anticyclonic) air higher up. By 7 December, the two inversions were very close together. The final result was the London was at the bottom of a pool of cold stagnant air, with a very effective "lid" overhead. The atmosphere contained a great deal of water in the form of very small droplets. Nearly 4,000 people died.

Subsequent analysis has revealed that between 80 and 90 per cent of the increase in deaths of persons during and immediately after the fog was due to respiratory and cardio-vascular diseases, mainly of a chronic nature. Over 90 per cent of the increased deaths were in people over the age of 45, and between 60 and 70 per cent over the age of 65. Morbidity *q.v.* also increased. It was concluded that it was impossible to state that any one pollutant was the cause of death, but that the irritants mainly responsible were probably derived from the combustion of coal. The maximum recorded concentrations of sulphur dioxide was 1.34 ppm over a 48-hour period.

On 3–7 December 1962, another acute air pollution incident occurred in London. Persistent fog covered the greater part of the country and was particularly dense in the lower Thames valley. In London, concentrations of sulphur dioxide reached an hourly peak of 1.9 ppm, but pollution by smoke was distinctly lower than in the 1952 smog. The public was alerted by warnings broadcast on radio and television and by Press announcements; the aged and those suffering from chronic respiratory and cardiac disease were advised to stay indoors. Some 700 persons died in the Greater London area due to the effects of the smog, as compared with 4,000 in 1952. The progressive establishment of smoke control areas under the Clean Air Act of 1956 with a consequent reduction of smoke by domestic dwellings, combined with improvements effected by industry, could well have contributed to the lower mortality. There is, however, no really conclusive evidence on this point. Sulphur dioxide levels were certainly no lower than in the 1952 smog.

During the period 1952/66 the discharge of sulphur dioxide from chimneys in London increased by some thirty per cent. The interesting point is that the concentrations of sulphur dioxide as measured by instruments at "breathing level" did not increase. As a large part of the increased tonnage discharged to atmosphere can be attributed to electricity generation from modern power stations, the net result is undoubtedly a tribute to the efficacy of the high chimneys currently employed.

Over the same period, the average annual concentration of sulphur dioxide in New York City rose significantly, although since 1966 it has fallen by about twenty five per cent due to increasingly severe restrictions on the amount of sulphur which fuels may contain. Air pollution episodes associated with an increase of morbidity and mortality occurred in New York City in 1953, 1958, 1963 and 1966. Upward trends in sulphur dioxide levels have been noted in Japan and elsewhere; however, in Moscow sulphur dioxide levels have fallen dramatically since a change-over to natural gas as the basic fuel.

Looping   The behaviour of a chimney plume in the presence of superadiabatic temperature lapse rates. Large-scale thermal eddies are set up and sporadic puffs of pollutants at high concentration may be brought to the ground at short distances for a few seconds. Looping occurs with light winds.

Los Angeles Smog   Smog of a photochemical *q.v.* nature, largely attributable to the effect of sunlight on motor vehicle exhaust gases. Basic to the Los Angeles control system is a programme of monitoring both weather conditions and levels of air contaminants. Three stages of alert related to the severity of exposure have been adopted, and appropriate control measures are instituted whenever necessary. In the first stage alert, all unnecessary activity which might pollute the air must be avoided. A second stage alert indicates a health menace, and the

County Air Pollution Control Director may impose limitation on the general operation of vehicles and may restrict the operations of public utilities and other industries to those essential to continued operation of the industrial complex. The third stage alert is evidence of a dangerous health menace and appropriate measures may be taken under the California Disaster Act to limit activities to emergency needs.

The smog problem of Los Angeles persisted after a drastic reduction of major stationary sources of air pollution; this left the motor vehicle as the major probable source. However the "cause and effect" mechanism was not at all easy to explain. During smogs considerable increases of ozone and oxidant material occur. The oxidant concentration that can cause eye irritation is regarded as being in the range 0.21 to 0.32 mg/m^3 (0.10 to 0.15 ppm), levels reached very frequently in Los Angeles. The highest value ever recorded in the city was 1.75 mg/m^3 (0.82 ppm) on 16 December 1966. These are not found in appreciable concentrations at night but only during daylight hours, beginning to form simultaneously throughout the Los Angeles basin in smoggy air shortly after dawn.

These facts suggested a photochemical formation of ozone or oxidants from air impurities by the action of sunlight. Sulphur dioxide, nitrogen dioxide and aldehydes absorb ultraviolet radiation in the wave lengths present at ground level and react in their excited states with molecular oxygen to produce atomic oxygen. Reactions with SO_2 and aldehydes are irreversible, but not so in the case of NO_2. In the latter case the absorption of ultraviolet light leads to the rupture of a bond to form atomic oxygen and nitric oxide. Reaction of the products with molecular oxygen leads to the formation of ozone and the regeneration of nitrogen dioxide. Thus NO_2 is available for the repetition of the process, unless converted to nitric acid or used up in organic substitution reactions. Hydrocarbons also play an essential part in this reaction, olefins being the most reactive.

Ozone formed during smog accounts for accelerated rubber cracking; while the oxidation of SO_2 to SO_3 with the formation of H_2SO_4 aerosol, as well as existing smoke, dusts and fumes, still further reduces visibility. Scientists in Los Angeles appear certain that the ozone and PAN (peroxyacetyl nitrate) in Los Angeles smogs have caused the serious decline in the citrus and salad crops in the area. Ozone and PAN produce eye irritation, coughing and chest soreness experienced by many Los Angeles residents on smoggy days. By 1953 it was established that the automobile was the largest source of air contaminants and the leading source of smog-forming hydrocarbons.

Photochemical pollution occurred in Melbourne, Australia, on a number of days between October 1973, and June 1974. Measurements of ozone showed that the World Health Organization Air Quality Goal (0.06 ppm, maximum for one-hour) and the United States Air Quality Standard (0.08 ppm, maximum for one hour, not to be exceeded once a year) were substantially exceeded on a number of occasions, the former on 28 days and the latter on 20 days.

L_x **Noise Levels** Noise levels in dBA which are exceeded for a specific percentage of the measurement period. For example, L_{10} and L_{90} noise levels mean that the noise level in dBA was exceeded for 10 per cent and 90 per cent of the measurement period, respectively. The Noise Advisory Council of the United Kingdom has recommended the adoption of the L_{10} index for measuring disturbance by traffic noise. It has recommended also that existing residential development should in no circumstances be subjected, as an act of conscious public policy, to more than 70 dBA on the L_{10} index unless some form of remedial or compensatory action is taken by the responsible authority.

Loudness The intensity of sound waves combined with the reception characteristics of the ear. Annoyance results from both the loudness and the frequency of a noise. Tones which stand out above the background noise, particularly those of high frequency, are usually the most annoying. Loudness depends on the response of the ear to sound and the ear is not equally sensitive at all frequencies.

M

Macronutrients Mineral nutrients utilized by organisms in large quantities, e.g. carbon, hydrogen, oxygen, nitrogen, phosphorous, sulphur, potassium, and calcium. *See* Micronutrients.

Mad Hatters Disease A disease suffered by hatters of a century ago who became mentally deranged as a result of absorbing mercury *q.v.* used in making felt for hats.

Main Sewer A sewer serving as the collector for a sizable district.

Maintenance The continuation of a species *q.v.* at a particular population *q.v.* density in a given habitat *q.v.* through reproductive behaviour alone.

Make Up Water Water supplied to replenish that lost in a system by leaks, evaporation, bleedoff, blowdown, withdrawal, etc.

Mallee Scrub A scrub consisting largely of low eucalyptus bushes characteristic of the dry sub-tropical region of southeast and southwest Australia.

Malthusian Theory of Population A theory of population developed by Thomas R. Malthus (1766–1834) and published in *An Essay on the Principle of Population* in 1798. The essence of the theory may be summarized as follows:

a) That population would soon outstrip the means of feeding it, if it were not kept down by vice, misery or self-restraint

b) That in a state of society where self-restraint does not act at all, or only acts so little that we need not think of it, population will augment until the poorest class of the community have only just enough to support life

c) That in a community where self-restraint may act eventually, each class of the community will augment until it reaches the point at which it begins to exercise that restraint.

Population, Malthus declared, tended to increase in a geometrical progression, whereas the means of subsistence increased in only arithmetical progression. The Essay was recast in a second edition in 1803; in this the author somewhat modifies his gloomy forbodings, hoping that personal restraint might prove an effective factor in the check to an increasing population.

Mangroves Plant communities and trees that inhabit tidal swamps, muddy silt and sand banks at the mouths of rivers and other low-lying areas which are regularly inundated by the sea, but which are protected from strong waves and currents. Mangroves are the only woody species which will grow where the land is periodically flooded with sea water; individual species have adapted themselves to different tidal levels, to various degrees of salinity and to the nature of the mud or soil. Mangroves vary in size from substantial trees up to thirty metres in height down to miniature forms less than waist high. Mangrove swamps and thickets support hundreds of terrestrial, marine and amphibian species. There is reason to believe that many edible marine fish depend on mangrove vegetation, or on the related 'wetlands' between shore and sea, for food and shelter at some stage of their life-cycles. A small mangrove area on Tallebudgera Creek in Queensland provides a feeding ground for fish and has been declared a fisheries reserve. Considerable areas of mangroves have been destroyed in recent years, both in Australia and elsewhere, to make way for industrial and housing development, harbours, marine and aircraft runways. Mangroves occur on many of the estuarine rivers and many of the bays and inlets of the northern and eastern coasts of Australia, essentially from Derby in Western Australia to the Clarence River in New South Wales, with scattered occurrences elsewhere.

Manhole A vertical shaft from the surface to the sewer and used for inspection, cleaning, and repair of the system.

Marginal Social, and Private Net Products Concepts associated with the name of the Cambridge economist A. C. Pigou (1877–1959), the marginal social net product is the total net product of physical things, or objective services, due to the marginal increment of resources in any given use or place, no matter to whom any part of this product may accrue. The marginal private net product is that part of the total net product of physical things, or objective services, due to the marginal increment of resources in any given use or place which accrues in the first instance, i.e. prior to sale, to the person responsible for investing resources there. Pigou's thesis was that, in general, industrialists are interested not in the social, but only in the private, net product of their operations. Self-interest will tend to bring about equality in the values of the marginal private net products of resources invested in different ways, but it will not tend to bring about equality in the values of the marginal social net products, except when marginal private net product and marginal social net product are identical. When there is a divergence between these two sorts of marginal net product, self-interest will not, therefore, tend to make the national dividend a maximum. Such divergences between the social and private net product are likely to occur even under conditions of simple competition. Pigou's view stands in sharp relief to the opinions of the Classical School. For example, David Ricardo said, "Where there is free competition, the interests of the individual and that of the community are never at variance." Pigou envisaged that when social and private net products differed, they should be brought into equality by government action (e.g. by appropriate taxation).

See Economic Welfare.

Marine Park   An extension of the terrestrial national park idea to the undersea world — a permanent reservation of part of the sea-bed. Marine parks exist in the United States, Japan, the Philippines, Kenya, Israel and Australia. Two marine national parks have been declared on the Great Barrier Reef *q.v.*

Marl   A calcareous clay; or mixture of clay and particles of calcite or dolomite, usually fragments of shells.

Maximum Permissible Body Burden   The total body content of a radioisotope which, if maintained, will not deliver to any critical organ a dose greater than the maximum permissible.

Maximum Permissible Concentration   The concentration of a radioisotope in air, water, milk, etc., which will deliver not more than the maximum permissible dose to a critical organ when breathed or consumed at a normal rate.

Maximum Permissible Dose   The dose of ionizing radiation accumulated in a specified time, of such magnitude that no bodily injury may be expected to result inthe lifetime of the person exposed and no intolerable burden is likely to accrue to society through genetic damage to his descendants.

Maximum Permissible Level   A term used loosely to refer to the maximum permissible dose-rate of radiation, the maximum permissible concentration of a radioisotope or the maximum permissible degree of contamination of a surface.

Megalopolitan Corridor   A term applied to the whole region between Washington, D.C. and Boston, U.S.A., and similar developments elsewhere.

Melanism   In moths, descriptive of increased dark pigmentation of the wings and other parts of the insect; usually melanism is controlled genetically. 'Industrial melanism', or adaptation to a dark, dirty, background, is brought about through natural selection *q.v.* The phenomenon was first noted in England about the middle of the nineteenth century. However, while the black form of the peppered moth was rare in Manchester in 1848, some 50 years later it comprised 95 per cent of the Manchester moth population. By the 1950s, the light-coloured form of the peppered moth could no longer be found; as air pollution has been reduced, the lighter forms have re-appeared. The blackness of the melanic moth has been of great value in protecting it from predatory birds while at rest on contaminated surfaces — a selective advantage in grimy areas.

Mercaptans   Organic compounds having the general formula R—SH, meaning that the thiol group, —SH, is attached to a radical such as CH_3 or C_2H_5. The simpler mercaptans have strong, repulsive, garlic-like odours; odours become less pronounced with increasing molecular weight and higher boiling points. Ethyl mercaptan, C_2H_5SH, is a liquid of nauseous odour although readily oxidized to ethyl disulphide by exposure to air. Mercaptans may be produced in oil refinery feed preparation units as a result of incipient cracking; the offensive gases are burnt in plant heaters. Mercaptans arising in cracking units are removed by scrubbing with caustic soda, the mercaptans being removed from the spent caustic soda by stream stripping and subsequently burned in a process furnace.

Mercury   A heavy liquid metal obtained generally from the roasting of mercuric sulphide ore (cinnabar). Mercury is used in older chlor-alkali plants, mercurial catalysts, the pulp and paper industry, seed treatment, and is released to the environment also in the burning of fossil fuels, and mining and refining processes. Mercury compounds may function as a cumulative poison affecting the nervous system (particularly in the form of methyl mercury, produced by the microbial conversion of inorganic mercury and some mercury-containing organic compounds). A normally harmless trace element, mercury may concentrate in food chains, particularly in fresh water and marine organisms. An epidemic outbreak of methyl mercury poisoning following ingestion of polluted shellfish and fish has occurred in Japan, associated with some fatal cases and congenital disease. This has been closely linked with heavy industrial pollution in Minamata Bay. A subsequent reduction in fish consumption has adversely affected Japan's large fishing industry. The presence of unacceptable levels of mercury in flake (school shark) has led to a reduction in the marketing of flake in Victoria. The presence of mercury does not necessarily indicate a condition of pollution; mercury in the ocean, for example, is largely of natural origin. Generally, inorganic salts of mercury are not a threat to living creatures, and are widely used in agriculture to control disease and pests; in contrast, organic compounds used to control fungal diseases in seeds and growing plants, fruits and vegetables, can be absorbed by humans and are extremely toxic. Alkyl mercury may cause permanent mental retardation.

Mesoclimate A local climatic effect due to terrain extending in influence over several kilometres and vertically one or two hundred metres, contrasting with the regional or macroclimate.

Mesophyte A plant which requires an average amount of moisture; in consequence most trees, shrubs, and herbs, living in climates of moderate rainfall and temperature are mesophytes.

Metabolism The sum of the total of the physical and chemical processes by which an organism converts simpler compounds into living, organized substance and then reconverts such material into simpler compounds with release of energy for its use.

Metalimnion *See* Thermocline.

Metamorphic Rock Rock which has changed character in response to pronounced changes in temperature, pressure, and chemical environment.

　See Igneous Rock, Sedimentary Rock.

Metamorphism ,The process by which consolidated rocks are altered in composition, texture, or internal structure by conditions and forces not resulting simply from burial and the weight of subsequently accumulated over-burden.

Meteorological Influences The effect of a range of atmospheric characteristics on the dispersal of pollutants, including heat. In respect of air pollution *q.v.*, the concentration of pollutants at or near ground level is a balance between the amount emitted and the degree to which it is diluted and dispersed by the atmosphere *q.v.*, or removed from the atmosphere by gravitation or precipitation. In a modern, industrial society it is only the enormous dilution produced by the atmosphere which renders the situation at all tolerable; without turbulence *q.v.* man could not live in large communities.

　The most important factor controlling the dispersal of pollution is turbulence. The intensity of turbulence depends on the following:

1. wind strength at a standard height
2. profile of wind variation with height
3. variation of wind direction with height
4. profile of temperature variations with height
5. rate at which heat is exchanged between the atmosphere and the ground and outer space
6. nature of the earth's surface
7. cloud formation, rain, etc.

Only in exceptional circumstances will high pollution levels be found when the wind is strong and possessing considerable turbulence. With low wind strengths and reduced turbulence pollution levels frequently increase, the most severe pollution occurs in non-turbulent conditions during an inversion *q.v.* when air temperature, instead of decreasing, increases with height.

　On the other hand, if the potential temperature gradient is positive, a condition of equilibrium will be reached at which the plume ceases to rise and travels horizontally in an atmosphere of density equal to its own. Vertical movement, whether upwards or downwards, is strongly inhibited and pollution remains near the level at which it was emitted or at the height to which it succeeded in penetrating. In these conditions an inversion is said to exist. This situation frequently arises on clear calm nights when the ground is cooled by outgoing radiation and the layer immediately above is colder than at higher levels. It also arises when a subsidence q.v. inversion occurs at a level well above the ground. In these conditions, plumes tend to follow a meandering path without change in height, a pattern called "fanning".

In a "neutral" atmosphere, in which air temperature falls slightly with height, dispersion of pollution is usually good. Plumes tend to follow a roughly conical path, a pattern known as "coning".

See Lapse Rates, Meteorology.

Meteorology The scientific study of the atmosphere q.v.; its structure, physical characteristics and phenomena. The atmosphere is regarded as consisting of several more or less concentric layers, the layer adjacent to the Earth's surface being the troposphere q.v., followed by the tropopause, stratosphere q.v., mesosphere and ionosphere q.v.

See Land-Breeze, Lapse Rates, Meteorological Influences, Prevailing Wind, Sea-Breeze, Wind Rose, Winds.

Methaemoglobinaemia The presence of methaemoglobin (a compound of haemoglobin q.v. and oxygen, more stable than oxyhaemoglobin) in the blood. It is produced by the action of oxidizing agents on the blood and gives rise in infants to the condition described as "blue baby". Between 1947 and 1950, Minnesota reported 139 cases of methaemoglobinaemia, including 14 deaths, caused by nitrate in farm well-water. Ruminant livestock have also become ill. The stomachs of infants and livestock reduce nitrate to nitrite which gives rise to this condition. Nitrites in natural waters are evidence of pollution, but will oxidize in due course to nitrates. Nitrates present in relatively high proportion to free ammonia indicate a well-treated effluent or a good natural recovery of water. As a result of the proven risk of nitrates becoming converted to nitrites in the stomach, the U.S. Public Health Service has imposed a limit of 10 ppm for nitrate in drinking water.

Methane   Often called marsh gas; an odourless, flammable gas that is the major constituent of natural gas. It develops in nature from decomposing organic matter, and is utilized in some sewage treatment plants for heating and power.

Methylene-Blue Stability Test   A test regarded as a means of assessing the stability of an effluent, stability being defined as the ability of an effluent to remain in an oxidized condition when incubated out of contact with air. The stability is determined not only by the content of biologically degradable material but also by the initial concentrations of dissolved oxygen *q.v.*, nitrate and nitrite, as well as by the type and quality of the microbial flora of the sample. The test lasts for 5 days at 20°C. If the blue colour persists after 5 days, the sample is considered stable.

Methyl Mercury   *See* Mercury.

Meuse Valley Incident   An air pollution incident of the 1930s involving respiratory illness and death. The topography of the Meuse Valley between Huy and Liége, a distance of some twenty-four kilometres, is that of a steep-sided trench about one kilometre wide and 120 metres deep. The valley is densely populated and is a centre of heavy industry. From 1—5 December 1930, prolonged stable weather conditions accompanied by the drainage of cold air (katabatic winds) from the uplands into the valley produced a severe inversion with heavy fog. Several hundred people became ill, and some sixty died as a result of respiratory illnesses. Many cattle had to be slaughtered.

An official enquiry begun within twenty-four hours of the end of the fog, put out a Report which concluded that the illnesses and deaths were caused by poisonous waste gas from many factories in the valley in conjunction with unusual climatic conditions. Although it had been impossible to identify any definite compound, sulphur dioxide was through to be the primary cause. A later investigation revealed that there were fifteen factories in the region which could have emitted gaseous fluorine compounds. The conclusion reached was that there was circumstantial evidence that illness was the result of acute fluorine intoxication aggravated by the immense quantities of suspended soot and particles in the atmosphere.

Microclimate A local climatic effect on a small scale from a metre to a kilometre horizontally and up to tree or house height. Vegetation, soil conditions, small-scale topography, structures and industrial activities, may create pronounced microclimatic differences.

Micronutrients Mineral nutrients utilized by organisms only in minute amounts, e.g. iron, boron, copper, manganese, zinc, molybdenum, and chlorine. *See* Macronutrients.

Micro-organisms Microscopic plants (bacteria, fungi, and algae) or animals (protozoa, rotifers, crustaceans, and nematodes) found in liquid wastes representing the active agents in biological treatment processes or the participants in the reduction activity.

Mineralization The microbial breakdown of humus *q.v.* and other organic material in soil *q.v.* to inorganic substances.

Mining Wastes Unwanted material arising from all classes of mining operations in two principal forms:

1. Rock waste, which may occupy valuable land and disfigure the landscape
2. tailings from mills, which as silt can impede the natural flow of streams.

Tailings may contain chemicals hazardous to vegetation and animal life. Modern mining methods utilize abandoned workings such as shafts, tunnels, and adits to store unwanted waste as backfill, thus conserving space. Great harm to stream life may occur where mill tailings have been piled in proximity to the drainage area of streams, e.g. copper and zinc compounds, lethal to fish, may be carried from the pile to the stream by rain-water. Filtrates may be carried for considerable distances underground to reach wells or other sources of water for livestock and human consumption. Sometimes, old tailing dumps are reworked to recover the metal content. Piles of tailings and other wastes may become mechanically unstable, when saturated with moisture, forming a mud flow that can damage property and life, as at Abafan in Wales.

Mixed Economy An economy in which resources are allocated partly through the decisions of private individuals and privately-owned business enterprises and partly through the decisions of government and state-owned enterprises. The two sectors are known as the private and public sectors, respectively.

See Laissez-faire, Planned Economy.

Molluscs Group of soft-bodied, unsegmented animals, usually with a hard shell such as shellfish.

Monitoring Programme The systematic deployment of measuring equipment for the purpose of detecting or measuring quantitatively or qualitatively the presence, effect, or level of any polluting substance. For example, the scientific measurement of pollution has gradually become recognized as an essential pre-requisite to remedial action. The measurement of the general atmospheric pollution to which people are constantly exposed is desirable for the following reasons:

1. It enables an objective assessment to be made. It is, however, important that measurements should be made in more than one type of district in an area, or a false impression may be obtained as to the amount of pollution to which the inhabitants are exposed.
2. It enables comparisons to be made with similar areas in other parts of the country.
3. The information gained assists in making an intelligent decision as to the remedial measures necessary and their order of priority.
4. It provides a means of judging the success of remedial measures once applied.
5. The information is useful to an air pollution control agency considering plans for the industrial, commercial and residential development of an area.
6. Knowledge of existing background levels of pollution is indispensable to the making of decisions in relation to chimney height proposals.
7. Facts concerning existing pollution are an essential ingredient in an Authority's campaign to convince the public of the need for a remedial programme.
8. A quantitative picture of the pattern of air pollution throughout the country is a valuable aid to medical investigations into the relationship between air pollution and disease.

9. It enables increases in air pollution that will result from industrial development in a given area to be predicted.

Monoculture The cultivation of a single crop, to the exclusion of other possible land uses.

Morbidity Rate The incidence of sickness in a population *q.v.*

Morphology The study of the form, structure, and origin, of organisms or earth features.
See Geomorphology.

Mortality Rate The rate of removal of individuals from a population *q.v.* by death.

Mulch Any suitable soil-protecting material such as straw, plastics or paper; one of the methods of checking wind erosion is to plant suitable grasses and to enable them to live through the dry season by covering them with mulch.

Mutagens Agents capable of modifying genes, the materials of heredity.

Mutation A transmissable change in the structure of a gene or chromosome.

Myxomatosis A disease of rabbits, caused by a virus and marked by fever, inflammation, and often death. It destroyed immense numbers of rabbits in Australia from 1950—51 onwards; as the disease has continued to affect the rabbit population, the aggregate consequent gain to the wool industry has been very substantial. The rabbit population today is only a fraction of its pre-myxomatosis level. Regarded as a pest uncontrollable by any other means, the C.S.I.R.O. introduced the disease to the wild rabbit population.

N

Natality Rate The rate of addition of new individuals to a population *q.v.* by birth.

National Estate Those components of the cultural and natural environment which are of such value to the nation or any part of it, that they should be conserved, managed and presented for the benefit of the community as a whole. Some components, such as the Great Barrier Reef *q.v.*, clearly belong to the heritage of the world also.

Components possess aesthetic, historical, scientific, social, cultural, ecological or other special values and include parks and reserves, beaches and coastlines, certain forests, rare species, buildings and gardens of special merit, sites of archaeological interest, scenic aspects of routes, urban areas of social character, museums, art treasures, areas of major wilderness, potential and rare ecosystems.

Measures to protect the national estate include planning controls and schemes, special funds to finance or subsidize acquisitions and other necessary conservation work, research and investigation into the effects of developments of various kinds, and tax and rating concessions. A National Estate Commission has been suggested by a Committee of Inquiry as a source of advice to government and to administer national estate matters. The guiding principle is that the ownership of land and property in a modern society implies a limited right only to the use and enjoyment of that land and property; hence mining operations, for example, must not harm or destroy parts of the national estate.

National Park   A relatively large area of land set aside for its features of predominantly unspoiled natural landscape, flora *q.v.* and fauna *q.v.*, permanently dedicated for public enjoyment, education and inspiration and protected from all interference, other than essential management measures, so that its natural attributes are preserved.

The main principle of National Park management is preservation to the greatest possible extent of the natural condition of these parks. For example, there are five categories for the management of the National Parks in Queensland —

1. Primitive Areas

   Primitive areas are of substantial size with well defined natural boundaries within which development of roads, tracks or structures is not permitted, scientific work is discouraged, and commercial development (such as tourist resorts, beekeeping, grazing and commercial fishing) is completely excluded.

2. Primitive and Recreation Areas

   A primitive and recreation area resembles a primitive area, the major difference being sufficient development of walking tracks, shelter sheds and directional signs to enable public use and enjoyment of the area on foot. Vehicular access is not provided, but scientific work may be permitted.

3. Recreation Areas
   These are limited in size, not exceeding 400 acres or half the park area (whichever is less). Facilities for recreation in a natural setting (e.g. camping, picnicking and boating) and public access are provided. There were approximately 2,500,000 visits to Queensland National Parks in 1972. As the demand for this type of recreation is likely to outstrip the capacity of National Parks to cater for recreation without detracting from other National Park values, the Department of Forestry and other authorities are providing alternative bushland recreation areas.

4. Scientific Areas
   Scientific areas are preserved as samples of the natural environment for scientific study (which is allowed under permit). Minimum access and shelter facilities may be provided.

5. Historic Areas
   Measures considered necessary to preserve the historical significance of an historic area are permitted.

National Welfare   A general objective commonly pursued by nations which can only be defined in a particular case by means of a series of multiple sub-objectives. In times of military crisis, national welfare may become virtually synonymous with effective defence. Thus the weighting to be placed on sub-objectives will vary from time to time.

Natural Increase   The rate of population *q.v.* growth, determined by subtracting the mortality rate *q.v.* from the natality rate *q.v.*

Natural Pollutants
1. Substances of natural origin present in the earth's atmosphere which may, when present in excess, be regarded as air pollutants. These include:
   a) ozone formed photochemically and by electrical discharge;
   b) sodium-chloride, or sea salt
   c) nitrogen-dioxide, formed by electrical discharge in the atmosphere

    d) dust and gases of volcanic origin

    e) soil dust from dust storms

    f) bacteria, spores and pollens and

    g) products of forest fires.

2. As in the case of air, excessive contamination of water may arise from natural sources; pollution of this kind is often associated with adverse weather conditions and is intermittent in character. During a storm, silt, vegetable matter and manure may be washed into a river. The erosion of river banks and valley slopes can lead to significant pollution of this kind. The Mississippi, in its southern stretches is known as "Big Muddy". Drainage from peaty areas is liable to contain much vegetable matter and organic matter. An excessive growth of weeds and other vegetable life may take place in a stream or river caused an obstruction of the free flow of water; when such vegetable matter dies it can seriously deplete the amount of dissolved oxygen in the river or stream. Acidic drainage from coal mines into rivers is due to ground water drainage through pyrites; the Monongahela River, Ohio, receives and carries into the Ohio River the equivalent of some 200,000 tons of sulphuric acid each year; this acid load from mine drainage travels for some 275 kilometres before it is completely neutralized.

See Air Pollution, Water Pollution.

Natural Resource Any portion of the natural environment — such as air, water, soil *q.v,* forest, wildlife. *q.v.* and minerals.

Natural Selection The agent of evolutionary change by which the organisms possessing advantageous adaptations in a given environment *q.v.* produce more offspring than those lacking such adaptations.

Nature Conservation The main purpose of this type of conservation is to preserve more or less natural plant communities (and possibly modified vegetation as well, in some instances) as representative examples of their kind.

    See Economic Conservation.

Nearctic Region The biogeographical region comprising North America above the tropics.

Negative Price A concept used in economic studies; an

imputed price for, for example, unwanted waste products. There is a strong underlying similarity between the concepts of negative prices and effluent taxes; the latter are a possible alternative to subsidies and standard setting as a means of controlling air and water pollution.
See Effluent Charge.

Neighbourhood Noise A term used by the British Noise Advisory Council to cover a great variety of sources of noise q.v. which may, and frequently do, cause disturbance and annoyance to the general public in their homes and going about their lawful occasions. They include, for example:
1. factory noise
2. noise from demolition, construction and road works
3. noise from ventilation and air-conditioning plant in buildings of all kinds
4. noise from sports, entertainment and advertising and
5. human noise arising from lack of consideration for others (loudspeakers, noisy parties, slamming of car doors, farewell hooting, and the like).
The term does not embrace industrial noise as it affects workers, aircraft noise and traffic noise.

Neotropical Region The biogeographical region comprising tropical North America and South America.

Neritic Zone The relatively warm, nutrient-rich, shallow-water zone overlying the continental shelf q.v.; the marine counterpart of the littoral zone q.v. of a lake. Terminating at the edge of the continental shelf, sunlight normally penetrates to the ocean bottom, permitting photosynthetic activity and promoting the growth of a vast population q.v. of floating and anchored plants. The total amount of biomass q.v. supported by the neritic zone is greater per unit volume of water than in any other part of the ocean.
See Abyssal Zone, Euphotic Zone.

Net Productivity See Gross Productivity.

Net Reproduction Rate The average number of female babies that will be born to a representative newly born female in her lifetime, if existing reproduction and mortality rates continue. If each 1,000 girls born in 1970 ultimately produce 1,600 female babies, the net reproduction rate will be 1.6 . A net reproduction rate

permanently greater than 1 means ultimate population *q.v.*
growth, although this may be deferred if the existing age
structure is unfavourable to growth; conversely, a net
reproduction rate less than 1 means ultimate population
decline. Between 1935 and 1939, the net reproduction
rate in Australia was 0.98; in 1963 it was 1.56 while in
more recent years the rate has tended to decline.

Niche   A place in the whole ecological system that provides
all the living needs of a species *q.v.*, that species being
better adapted to occupy that niche than any other species.

Night-soil   Human excrement or faecal matter and human
urine.

Nitrification   The microbial conversion of ammonium and
nitrite compounds to nitrates, generally by soil nitrifying
bacteria.

Nitrilotriacetic Acid (NTA)   A proposed substitute for
phosphate as a "builder" in detergents *q.v.* However,
reservations about potential harm to the environment of
this alternative has prevented its adoption. A typical
detergent may contain as much as 50 per cent phosphate
(commonly sodium tripolyphosphate).

Nitrogen Cycle   The circulation of nitrogen atoms brought
about mainly by living things. An essential ingredient of
proteins required by all living organisms, nitrogen enters
the living part of the biogeochemical cycle in two different
ways:

1. Atmospheric nitrogen is converted into nitrogen
   compounds which can be utilized by plants and animals
   through nitrogen fixation effected by certain nitrogen-
   fixing bacteria and certain blue-green algae

2. the excrements of animals and dead bodies of animals
   and plants contain very complex nitrogen compounds
   which are broken down by ammonifying bacteria in the
   soil and converted into ammonia.

Some bacteria ("nitrifying" bacteria) convert ammonia by
oxidation into nitrates, while other bacteria oxidize the
nitrites into nitrates. Amongst the factors considered
essential for nitrification to proceed are the presence of
phosphates, oxygen and a base (e.g. sodium or calcium) to
neutralize the nitrous and nitric acids. The final oxidation
product, nitrate, is utilized by plants for building up plant

proteins. Both ammonia and nitrates can be easily assimilated by plants. Finally, a further group of denitrifying bacteria break up nitrogen compounds and release free nitrogen into the atmosphere, completing the nitrogen cycle.
See Biogeochemical Cycles.

Nitrogen Oxides Oxides formed and released in all common types of combustion; they are formed by the oxidation of atmospheric nitrogen at high temperatures. Introduced into the atmosphere from automobile exhausts, furnace stacks, incinerators and other similar sources, the oxides include nitrous oxide, nitric oxide, nitrogen dioxide, nitrogen pentoxide, and nitric acid. Nitrogen dioxide can be injurious to health when inhaled; nitric acid being produced on the lung tissue with the moisture in the lungs. Nitric oxide can combine with the haemoglobin of the blood to form an addition complex. The oxides of nitrogen undergo many reactions in the atmosphere; emissions from motor vehicle exhausts are important in the atmospheres of Los Angeles, Tokyo, and some eastern seaboard Australian cities, when in the presence of sunlight and hydrocarbons they catalyse the formation of the irritant, ozone. Measures are being widely introduced to restrict the formation of oxides of nitrogen in motor vehicle exhaust gases and boiler-plants.
See Los Angeles Smog.

Noise Sound which is not wanted by the recipient. It is clear that what may be a pleasant and enjoyable sound to one person may not be to another. Beauty, in this case, may be said to be in the ear of the listener. The various sources of environmental noise may be divided into separate categories: Road traffic; Industry and commerce; Domestic and residential; Construction and demolition work; Road repair and maintenance work; Entertaining, advertising and sporting activities; Extractive industries; Aircraft.
See Neighbourhood Noise.

Noise and Number Index (NNI) An index for the measurement of disturbance from aircraft noise; developed in the United Kingdom in 1961 and since used extensively. The index was based on a social survey carried out around

Heathrow Airport for the Wilson Committee, and takes into account the average peak noise level at the ground due to passing aircraft and also the number of aircraft which fly past. Local planning authorities have been advised to take aircraft noise into account in considering planning applications. The Surrey County Council has evolved a land-use zoning scheme, based on NNI contours, to control development around Gatwick Airport.

Noise Exposure Forecast (NEF)   A technique for predicting the subjective effect of aircraft noise on the average person, exposure levels being expressed in NEF units. Factors which are taken into consideration are the frequency of aircraft movements and their distribution by day and night; the magnitude and duration of aircraft noise as determined by type, weight and flight profile; and the distribution of the noise energy over the spectrum of audible frequencies. In applying the NEF technique, a pattern of contour lines is drawn on the map of the area surrounding the airport.

Noise Rating   A system whereby manufacturers indicate on their products the noise level emitted at a fixed distance from the appliance.

Noise Zoning   The statutory classification of areas according to usage; this method allows higher noise levels in areas where their effect will not be noticed but maintains lower levels in more sensitive areas such as suburban residential sites and rural areas. An inherent problem in zoning lies in the difficulty of accurately defining the zones and of setting the boundaries between adjacent zones. Noise zones are not necessarily compatible with established land-use zones.

See Neighbourhood Noise.

Non-renewable Resources   Natural resources which, once consumed, cannot be replaced e.g. a ton of coal once consumed is gone forever in that form. Mineral resources generally are regarded as wasting assets of this kind. However, it is difficult to predict what the consequences of exhausting particular resources would be. For any particular mineral the exhaustion process would be gradual, accompanied, *ceteris paribus*, by a steady rise in its price. A rising relative price intensifies exploration and ensures treatment of lower grades of ore; recycling and reclamation of scrap and residues are also encouraged. Meanwhile developments in substitute materials and processes and in the pattern of demand could mean that a mineral considered "indispensable" at one stage could become redundant at another.

Nuclear Fission The splitting of the nucleus *q.v.* of a heavy atom into two fragments of approximately equal mass, usually by neutron bombardment.

See Nuclear Reactor.

Nuclear Reactor An assembly in which a fission chain reaction is caused to take place in a controlled manner. The essential components of a reactor are a fissile material for fuel, a moderator, a coolant and a neutron absorbent material to act as a control for the neutron flux in the reactor core.

See Nuclear Fission.

Nucleus The central core of the atom composed of protons and neutrons.

Nuclide The nucleus of an isotope.

Nutrient Budget An estimate for a particular living system setting out the amounts of essential mineral nutrients which are taken up or lost.

Nutrients *See* Eutrophication.

Nutrient Stripping A tertiary treatment *q.v.* of waste waters, either to reduce the rate of eutrophication *q.v.* of receiving waters or to permit the re-use of water for domestic purposes. Constituents of interest are those responsible for stimulating excessive growth of algae *q.v.*, namely compounds of phosphorous and nitrogen. Methods range from chemical coagulation to advanced treatment processes such as those developed for the desalination of seawater and brackish waters. The disposal of the concentrates arising in all advanced waste water treatment processes presents an additional problem.

O

Offensive Industry or noxious industry. Any business which by reason of the process involved, or the methods of manufacture, or the nature of the raw materials or goods used, produced or stored, is likely, as a result of the inadequacy of the available means of control, to cause effluvia, fumes and odours of a character offensive to persons on adjacent land. Historically, the "offensive trades" have included those dealing in the by-products of abattoirs, e.g. offal, blood, hides and bones, and the process for dealing with condemned meat and fish.

Oil Pollution   A pollution problem related mainly to the growth of the tanker trade and particularly with the development of giant tankers; statistics have shown that the incidence of oil spills at sea is increasing. The grounding of the *Oceanic Grandeur* in the Torres Strait in 1970 accelerated Australian thinking, and the need for a national plan to deal with the threat of damage to the coastal environment became recognized. A national plan has now been prepared; under it, dispersant material and spraying equipment have been provided at nine points around the Australian coastline, and responsibilities allocated. The plan has been published by the Commonwealth Department of Transport.

See 'Load-on-Top' System, Santa Barbara 'Blow-Out', Torrey Canyon Disaster. Also Figures 9 and 10.

Figure 9   Vikoma System for the containment of oil spills at sea. Developed by B.P., the seaboom is about 500 metres in length. Once the boom has been inflated, it is towed downwind of the oil slick and formed into a U-shape; under the influence of wind, the oil becomes trapped within the boom. Skimming equipment travels into the boom enclosure and the oil is pumped into containers (Source: B.P. Australia Ltd., Melbourne, Victoria)

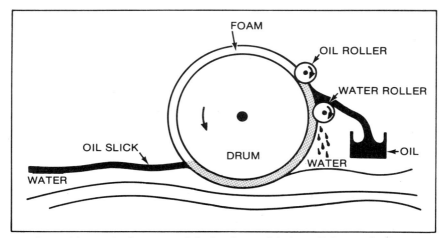

Figure 10 Craft-mounted device for reclaiming oil from a harbour or inland water way (Source: Welles Products Corporation, Roscoe, Illinois)

Oligotrophic Applied to a body of water containing relatively low amounts of nutrients, and usually with considerable dissolved oxygen in the bottom waters.
    See Eutrophication.

Omnivore An organism which obtains energy from the consumption of both plants and animals.
    See Carnivore, Herbivore.

Open Cast Mining The working of coal seams near their outcrops, i.e. near the point at which coal appears at the surface. Generally, the actual outcrop edge of a seam is very inferior, due to prolonged oxidation.

Open Cut Mining or strip mining. A technique of mining employed when the coal is not more that about thirty metres below the surface; the overlying earth and rock are mechanically stripped to expose the coal which is then removed with or without blasting.

Opportunity-cost The real cost of satisfying a want, expressed in terms of the cost of the sacrifice of alternative activities. For example, if capital funds could earn 7 per cent elsewhere, then that is their cost in present use. If machinery has no alternative use whatsoever, the opportunity cost is zero; historical cost in this instance is irrelevant. The opportunity cost of factors currently obtained from outside the firm is measured by the price currently paid for their services. In the case of factors already owned by the firm, it is measured by the amount for which factors could be hired out or sold to another firm. If a government chooses to build more schools and finds it must cut down on its road construction programme, then the cost of the schools programme can be represented as so many kilometres of road.

Optimum Population   Originally conceived as the ideal size of population, which will yield the highest possible material return per head of population. As Cannan expressed it: "The optimum for population is the right movement which will give the largest return to industry in the long run, the interests of the people of all generations being taken into account". The optimum for population would thus be related to the available supplies of other factors of production; it would therefore change with changes in the supply of other factors. Today the concept would be broadened into one in which the general welfare of the population is maximized.

See Human Progress Index, Quality of Life.

Ord River Irrigation Scheme   A scheme providing for the construction of a diversion dam, a main irrigation channel and a pilot irrigation scheme at the Ord River, in the far north of Western Australia. After evaluating the results of the pilot scheme, the Commonwealth Government, amid considerable controversy about the economic viability and environmental effects of the project, agreed to provide finance for the construction of the main dam and reticulation of irrigation areas in Western Australia; the main dam was completed in late 1971, and water from it became available for irrigation in 1972. The rate of development of the scheme has been slowed down as a result mainly of difficulties in achieving economic viability with the crops grown in the area.

Oriental Region   The biogeographical region comprising tropical Asia and western Indonesia.

Organochlorine Insecticides   *See* Chlorinated Hydrocarbon Insecticides.

Organophosphorus Insecticides   A diverse group of non-persistent synthetic chemical poisons which act chiefly on the nervous system; the group includes fenthion, malathion, and parathion.

Outfall Sewer A pipe or conduit used to transport either raw sewage, or treated effluent, to a final point of discharge into a body of water, e.g. the outfall sewer from the Carrum treatment plant that discharges into the ocean off Cape Schank, Victoria.

Oxidation Pond A shallow lagoon *q.v.* or basin within which waste water is purified, through sedimentation and both aerobic and anaerobic biochemical activity over a period of time; used in favourable climates.

Oxygen Absorbed (OA) The amount of oxygen in parts per million absorbed by a sample of water from acidic permanganate in 4 hours at $27°$ C.

Oxygen Sag Curves Graphical curves which relate the dissolved oxygen content of water against time flow, within the context of the process of self-purification, following the discharge of pollutants into a stream.
See Figure 11.

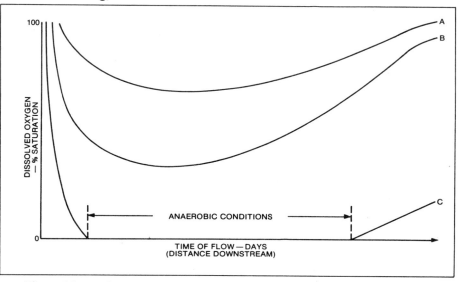

Figure 11   Oxygen sag curves relating dissolved oxygen content against time of flow. The three curves illustrate the de-oxygenation and recovery of a polluted stream after (A) slight, (B) heavy, and (C) gross pollution. At the bottom of each curve, the oxygen content is minimal.

Ozone A triatomic molecule of oxygen. Above minimal levels, it is an irritant to human beings and animals. It is a natural constituent of the atmosphere occurring in concentrations of about 0.01 ppm; the toxicity threshold for workers is 0.1 ppm. Ozone is produced by certain high voltage electrical equipment; it is also produced in certain circumstances when photochemical reactions occur in the atmosphere between ultraviolet light (sunlight) and the oxides of nitrogen and hydrocarbons emitted to the atmosphere by motor vehicles.
See Los Angeles Smog.

Ozonosphere A layer of the atmosphere between about twenty kilometres and 50 kilometres above the surface of the earth containing ozone *q.v.* The ozone is produced through the splitting of some oxygen molecules, the resulting atomic oxygen recombining with unaffected molecules to yield ozone (O_3).

P

Package Treatment Plant A compact, transportable, factory-made, sewage treatment *q.v.* unit capable of achieving a specific effluent quality; it may be deployed to serve a housing estate for a temporary period prior to the installation of a trunk sewer. This technique has been employed by the Melbourne and Metropolitan Board of Works.

Palaearctic Region The biogeographical region that includes Europe, Asia north of the Himalayas, northern Africa and northern Arabia.

Paleoecology The study of relationships between ancient organisms and their environments.

Palynology The study of pollens and spores in a historical context through observations on pollen grains and other spores preserved in ancient peat and sedimentary deposits; the findings are widely used to interpret past environmental conditions.

Parathion A highly toxic material used as an insecticide; it is effective as a contact and stomach poison against many species *q.v.* Special precautions are necessary to prevent inhalation and skin contamination.

See Organophosphorus Insecticides.

Pathogenic Organisms Organisms responsible for the transmission of communicable diseases such as cholera, bacillary dysentery, typhoid fever, typhus fever, bacterial food poisoning, malaria, yellow fever, amoebic dysentery and infective hepatitis. Wide varieties of pathogenic bacteria, viruses and parasites responsible for food and water-borne-diseases are involved.

See Coliform Bacteria, Virus.

Pathological Waste Infectious or potentially infectious waste, the disposal of which could be a public health hazard or nuisance; it includes hospital wastes, some laboratory wastes, and any other material infected with bacteria and viruses.

Pelagic Relating to communities of marine organisms which belong to the open sea, living free from direct dependence on bottom or shore, i.e. belonging to that part of the ocean which is deeper than the littoral zone *q.v.* although shallower than the abyssal zone *q.v.*

Percolating Filter or trickling filter. A bed of inert material provided with means of distributing sewage *q.v.* over the surface. The surface of the medium becomes covered with a film of micro-organisms which effectively purify the sewage under aerobic *q.v.* conditions.

Permafrost Perennially frozen ground.

Peroxyacetyl Nitrates (PAN) A component of photochemical smog and the primary plant toxicant of smog-type injury; field levels of 0.01 to 0.05 ppm will injure sensitive plants. Causes eye irritations and other health effects.

See Los Angeles Smog.

Persistence An important characteristic of a pollutant in an environmental medium (air, water, or soil) or in living tissue; substances that persist (remain active for a long time) in a toxic form, such as certain heavy-metal metabolites, organo-chlorine compounds, and polychlorinated biphenyls (PCBs) are particularly hazardous.

Pesticides Collective name for a variety of insecticides, fungicides, herbicides, fumigants, and rodenticides. Of these compounds, synthetic organic chemicals are the most important, in terms both of growth rate, of consumption and potential for contaminating the environment. Synthetic organic pesticides are produced, usually, as concentrated materials which are later 'formulated' before application. Formulation consists of mixing the concentrated material with such diluents as clays, talcs, water, kerosine and other solvents. The purpose of formulation is to assist the even distribution of a small amount of active chemical over a large area at a pre-determined rate per unit of area. Pesticidal dusts, granules, solutions, emulsions and suspensions are applied by aircraft or by ground equipment. Pesticides may be detected in water, soil, and food (including milk, meat, fruits, and fish living in polluted waters) particularly in rural areas where they are widely used for agricultural purposes. Insecticides may be classified as:

1. Chlorinated hydrocarbon (organo-chlorine) types
2. Organo-phosphorus types
3. Carbamates and others.

By and large, environmental pollution by pesticides in Australia is minimal. Intensive agricultural production occupies only 0.08 per cent of the surface area of the country, and there is limited need or incentive to apply pesticides on rangeland pasture or grain crops. A large proportion of the insecticides used is for controlling parasites on sheep and cattle. The sale of pesticides is strictly regulated under State laws that require products to be registered and all label directions approved. No new pesticide may be registered without positive evidence of its safety to people, crops, domestic animals, wildlife, and the environment generally. Pesticide residues in raw agricultural commodities are monitored by the Commonwealth Department of Primary Industry and in the total diet by the National Health and Medical Research Council.

See Carbamates, Chlorinated Hydrocarbon Insecticides, Organophosphorus Insecticides.

pH The measure of the degree of acidity or alkalinity of an effluent. Unpolluted rivers generally vary in pH value from about 5.0 (acid moorland peaty streams) to about 8.5 (chalk streams). Acid water draining from an abandoned coal mine may have a pH value as low as 2.0; this drainage water is actually a sulphuric acid solution. In order that the normal biological and chemical processes which occur in a river or during sewage treatment should not be adversely affected, the river water or sewage should not vary greatly from neutral, i.e. pH 7.0. For this reason river authorities usually set limits between pH 6.0 to pH 9.0, and sewage authorities between pH 5.0 and pH 10.0 . pH values normally vary between pH 5.0 (acid) and pH 8.5 (alkali).

Phenotype   The sum of the characteristics displayed by an organism, as contrasted with the set of genes possessed by it.

See Genotype.

Philoprogenitive   Producing abundant offspring; prolific.

Phosphates   Essential nutrients for plants and normal constituents of the food of man and animals. The principal man-made sources are sewage, agricultural run-off, and detergent "builders". In excessive amounts it is considered a major factor in the process of eutrophication *q.v.* resulting in excessive growth of aquatic plants, depletion of oxygen, loss of fish and general degradation of water quality.

Phosphorus Cycle   The circulation of phosphorus atoms brought about mainly by living things. Phosphorus is an essential element in ribonucleic (RNA) and desoxyribo-nucleic (DNA) acids which are the bearers of genetic information and play other important parts in the processes which take place in living cells. Phosphorus becomes available to plants from a variety of natural and artificial sources. The process of decay releases phosphates to the soil and completes the phosphorus cycle.

See Biogeochemical Cycles.

Photochemical   Pertains to the permanent, chemical effects of the interaction of radiant energy (especially light) and matter.

See Los Angeles Smog.

Photosynthesis   The formation in chloropyll-containing (green) plants of carbohydrates from atmospheric carbon dioxide and water; simultaneously free oxygen is released into the atmosphere *q.v.* The energy needed for photosynthesis is supplied to green plants by solar energy *q.v.*

Phreatophyte   A plant with roots long enough to reach the water-table *q.v.* and hence draw its water from the ground-water *q.v.* supply.

Phylogeny   The evolutionary history of a group of organisms, as distinct from the development of the individual organism.

Phylum   The evolutionary tree which results from inheritance and the mutation-selection process; a principle division of the animal or the vegetable kingdom.

Phytobentos   Higher acquatic plants fixed to the ground. This type of flora is divided into hydatophytes (plants immersed in water); amphiphytes (amphibious plants); and marsh plants. Through the process of photosynthesis *q.v.*, the surrounding water is freed from carbon dioxide and supplied with free oxygen.

Phytophagus   Descriptive of animals that feed on plants, i.e. herbivorous animals.

Phytoplankton   The primary basis of animal life in the sea consisting of passively floating minute plants, chiefly diatoms (microscopic unicellular brownish algae). Phytoplankton accomplishes the photosynthesis *q.v.* for which it needs solar energy *q.v.* that penetrates only the upper layer of the sea. Many ocean fish feed on phytoplankton which is also the basic food of zooplankton *q.v.*

Phytotoxicant   Poisonous to plants.

Pica   Unnatural craving for the consumption of non-food substances.

Picloram   A powerful and persistent weedicide. It has been used in Australia to control the regrowth of unwanted woody species, e.g. eucalypts in pastures. Picloram is extremely toxic to legumes, but in concentrations of well under one part per million.

Pisciculture   The culture of growing of fish.

Pitch   The frequency of a tone or sound, depending on the relative rapidity of the vibrations by which it is produced. In low frequency sounds, the vibrations are relatively far apart; in high frequency sounds they are close together. While the greater the frequency, the higher the pitch of a sound, the relationship is not a linear one.

   See Sound Wave.

Plankton Animals and plants of minute size which float in the waters of seas, rivers, ponds, and lakes; these organisms are largely incapable of independent movement and are passively transported by water currents and wave action. They frequently impart a faint greenish-brown cast to the water. Plankton are divisible into:
1. Plants (chiefly algae *q.v.*) known as phytoplankton *q.v.*; and
2. Animals (primarily crustaceans and protozoa) known as zooplankton *q.v.*

Planned Economy An economy in which the problems of production, distribution and growth are resolved by a central planning authority.
  See Laissez-Faire, Mixed Economy.

Planning The plotting of a course of action. Planning may be merely "indicative", involving the collection, processing and distribution of information for others responsible for policy-making and executive action; or it may be "normative", actually involving executive action or enforcement.
  See Planned Economy.

Planning Permission A provision of town and country planning legislation that no development or change in the existing use of land or buildings may be made without the approval or 'planning permission' of the appropriate planning authority.

Pleistocene The geological epoch preceding the Holocene (or Recent) in the Quaternary period, which lasted from about one and a half million years ago until ten thousand years ago. During the Pleistocene epoch, four major ice ages occurred.
  See Geological Time Scale.

Polluter Pays Principle A principle which equates the price charged for use of environmental resources with the cost of damage inflicted on society by using them. The price charged may be levied directly, e.g. as taxes on the process which generates pollution or as the purchase price of licences which entitle the holder to generate specific quantities of pollutants. If the producer or consumer can avoid the additional expense, he will attempt to do so; there is, therefore, an incentive to refrain from using the polluting item or to change consumption patterns or production processes in ways which mitigate pollution. Alternatively, in a reversal of principle, measures may take the form of direct payments from the public purse to polluters not to pollute. The difficulty with either procedure is to decide the "right" price to charge, or the "right" subsidy to pay; both involve an assessment of the monetary value of a clean and unimpaired environment. For this reason, non-market techniques of pollution control are frequently preferred; under the "polluter pays" principle, non-market measures encompass the promulgation of regulations governing in various ways the emission or effects of pollution. Regulations eliminate some of the uncertainty which is inherent in market approaches. As a member of the Organization for Economic Co-operation and Development, Australia adopted the guiding principles of that organisation in respect of the economic aspects of the environmental policies, including the "polluter pays" principle. The principle was re-affirmed by Australia at the U.N. Conference on the Human Environment held in Stockholm in 1972. However, an examination of the practices of members of the Organization for Economic Co-operation and Development reveals that a majority provide some incentive to industry to install pollution control equipment. Canada, France, Japan and the U.S.A. all provide incentives to stimulate industrial concerns to install air pollution control equipment.

See Licences, Tax Incentives.

Pollution Any direct or indirect alteration of the physical, thermal, biological, or radioactive properties of any part of the environment *q.v.* by discharging, emitting, or depositing wastes or substances so as to affect any beneficial use *q.v.* adversely, to cause a condition which is hazardous or potentially hazardous to public health, safety or welfare, or to animals, birds, wildlife, fish or aquatic life, or to plants.

Polychlorinated Biphenyls (PCBs) The products of the chlorination of the hydrocarbon compound, biphenyl. Theoretically there are 210 different compounds which can arise from this reaction. Since about 1930, they have been used in industrial applications. As produced and sold, the various grades of PCBs are all mixtures of varying complexity, and for convenience are characterized by the percentage of chlorine which they contain. PCBs are chemically inert materials not hydrolyzed by water, and resistant to alkalis, acids and other chemicals. They possess boiling points in the range 278° C to 451° C. Stable to long heating, they are insoluble in aqueous media but highly soluble in hydrocarbons *q.v.* They are not easily decomposed by the temperatures associated with the destruction of rubbish by combustion. It is believed that they are even more stable than DDT and its metabolites and accordingly resistant to biodegradibility or biological decomposition; there is ample evidence which points to PCBs as being highly persistent chemicals which now contaminate much of our environment. Steps have been taken in several countries to restrict the use of PCBs, which have found use in transformers and capacitors, as heat transfer fluids, hydraulic fluids, and as plasticisers in paints, varnishes, adhesives, inks and sealants. Satisfactory substitutes are available in some areas. The use of PCBs as a heating transfer fluid led to a major accident in Japan in 1968; PCB leaked from a pipe in food processing equipment, resulting in the contamination of rice bran oil. This resulted subsequently in the poisoning of about one thousand people who ingested the contaminated oil. Even at concentrations as low as parts per billion or less, PCBs can be lethally toxic to some fish; however, they are only moderately toxic to birds and mammals.

Polycyclic Aromatic Hydrocarbons (PAH) A variety of chemical compounds such as benzopyrene, dibenzopyrene, dibenzoacridine, occupational exposure to which can cause cancer in man.

See Hydrocarbons.

Polythene polyethylene or high-pressure polythene: A compound of carbon and hydrogen. The products of complete combustion are carbon dioxide and water only.

Population A number of interacting and interbreeding organisms of the same species *q.v.* forming a group, separated more or less clearly from other groups of the same or other species; a discrete, dynamic unit of a species.

See Community, Density Dependent, Net Reproduction Rate.

Population, Declining   A population *q.v.* diminishing in size. In the case of a country, the effect will be to raise the average output per head only if the country was over-populated economically in the first place. Short of mass emigration, a declining population will only occur when the birth-rate falls below the death-rate. An unavoidable effect is the growth in the size of the dependent population consisting mainly of the older-age groups. For the working population, this implies a progressively increasing burden of welfare services. The smaller total market and labour force may mean that the full economies of large-scale production cannot be achieved. Industry would also experience greater difficulty in securing a transfer of labour from declining to expanding industries.

Population Dynamics   The study of variations in population density; the population density being the number of individuals of a population *q.v.* in a given space or area.

Population Ecology   The study of the laws governing the numbers of animals in relation to the areas that they inhabit; it takes into account, inter alia, the relationships of animals to their food, and to other sorts of animals that eat the same type of food. The term applies to the same field of inquiry as population dynamics *q.v.*

Population Explosion   A phenomenal increase in the rate of natural growth of the world population. While the time required for the population to double was about 1500 years during the period 8000 B.C. to 1650 A.D., it now takes only about 35—37 years. This rapid increase of population is due to a combination of the application of modern drugs and large scale public health measures (control of specific diseases and improved sanitation) which have depressed death-rates and extended the span of human life without any accompanying fall in birth rates. On the basis of present population trends, the United Nations Organization forecasts for the year 2000 a world population of between 5.5 and 7 thousand million people.

Potential Temperature, Gradient of   In the lowest layers of the atmosphere *q.v.* the difference between the adiabatic *q.v.* lapse rate and the actual atmospheric lapse rate. When the gradient of potential temperature is zero, the buoyancy of a mass of rising gas is constant and there is no theoretical ceiling. If the gradient is negative, the buoyancy of the gas will increase as it rises, and if it is positive it will decrease and there will be a height at which the buoyancy vanishes.

See Lapse Rates.

Poza Rica Incident An air pollution incident involving respiratory illness and death. At Poza Rica, Mexico, on 24 November 1950, some 22 persons died and 320 were hospitalized as a result of the malfunction of an oil refinery sulphur recovery unit; large quantities of hydrogen sulphide *q.v.* were vented to the atmosphere *q.v.* Meteorological data indicated that a pronounced low altitude temperature inversion *q.v.* prevailed at the time. Unlike otheracute air pollution incidents, a single source and air pollutant were responsible.

Precipitous Bluff An outstanding geological feature of the southwest wilderness of Tasmania, under threat of commercial exploitation for its limestone deposits. The top 300 metres of the bluff comprises dolerite, a hard brown-coloured rock of organ-pipe structure. It overlies softer sedimentary rocks including beds of limestone known as 'Gordon Limestone'.

Predator A creature or organism that lives on prey. In the "predator chain" the consumer at each successive trophic level *q.v.* is usually larger than the consumed animal. In a number of food chains, man is the final predator.

See Food Chain.

Preservation Keeping in existence unchanged, natural resources, structures or situations which have been inherited from the past.

Prevailing Wind That wind, indicated by direction, at a certain place or in a certain area, which has a considerably higher frequency than any other.

See Wind Rose.

Primary Treatment In respect of sewage treatment *q.v.*, a series of mechanical treatment processes which remove most of the floating and suspended solids, but which have a limited effect only on colloidal and dissolved material. Mechanical separation is achieved by screening, i.e. passing the sewage through a screen, the coarser materials being removed; screens usually consist of a series of parallel bars. Grit chambers or detritus tanks may also be provided; in effect they are long sedimentation chambers designed to maintain low velocities of flow. Inorganic matter readily separable from the sewage is removed in these chambers. Further separation may be brought about in sedimentation or settling tanks in which suspended solid matter is deposited; the raw sludge deposited is removed at frequent intervals by pump or hydrostatic pressure. The sludge removed passes into sludge digestion *q.v.* tanks for subsequent treatment. These initial treatment stages remove the grosser signs of sewage contamination, but the effluent still has a high demand for oxygen and is highly charged with potantially harmful bacteria.

See Secondary Treatment.

Producer   Autotrophic populations, often of green plants, which obtain energy from outside an ecosystem *q.v.* and direct it into the system. Within this context, primary productivity is the rate at which energy is taken into an ecosystem through the activity of producers.

Production Ecology   A study of the more complex "life communities" or biomes *q.v.* considered as trophic associations or food cycles; it is concerned essentially with the dynamic structure of the system whereby regulation is effected, rather than with the actual operation of the regulation processes on individuals within populations. The name "production ecology" results from an increasing preoccupation with the supply, or production, of food and ultimately with the flow, or exploitation, of energy within trophic cycles.

Productivity   *See* Gross Productivity.

Product Standard   Derived standards or working levels of pollutants applied to products such as food or detergents. The maximum acceptable level of potential pollutants in the specified product is designed to ensure that under specified circumstances primary and secondary ambient quality protection standards are not exceeded.

See Standard.

Production Residues   Wastes arising in production and distribution processes.

See also Consumption Residues.

Profundal Zone   The area immediately beneath the limnetic zone *q.v.* of a lake; it extends downwards to the lake bottom. The penetration of sunlight to the profundal zone is very limited, hence green plant life is absent. Bacteria and fungi flourish in bottom ooze.

Protozoa   A group, or phylum *q.v.*, of animals consisting of one cell only with at least one well-defined nucleus; it comprises the classes Flagellata, Ciliophora, Rhizopoda, and Sporozoa. The division is not always clear-cut, as both fungi and algae *q.v.* also include unicellular forms.

Psychosocial Stressors   Stimuli suspected of causing diseases which originate in social relationships or arrangements and affect the organism through the medium of the higher nervous processes.
See Stress.

Psychosomatic   Related to mind (psyche) and body (soma); descriptive of diseases arising from, or aggravated by, a mind-body relationship.

Pulverization   or milling or shredding. An intermediate step only in refuse *q.v.* disposal which consists in reducing refuse to small-size particles; it is particularly valuable in conjunction with transfer stations and land-fill *q.v.* methods, reducing the volume of refuse to be handled.

Pumping Station   An installation comprising a wet-well, pump, and pressure pipe, often located underground, operated for the purpose of raising sewage *q.v.* to a higher elevation. A pumping station, located at a low point in a catchment *q.v.*, may be used to despatch sewage to a treatment plant elsewhere.
See Sewage Treatment.

Putrefaction   Decomposition of organic matter in an anaerobic *q.v.* state releasing foul-smelling gases and incompletely oxidized products. It is important to distinguish between putrefaction and the process of anaerobic digestion *q.v.*; an anaerobic digestion process permanently removes the offensive odour of many organic wastes so that they can be used on agricultural land without causing nuisance.

Putrescible Wastes   Wastes which consist mainly of plant or animal residues and which undergo degradation by bacteriological action; e.g. abattoir refuse, animal residues, cannery wastes, fats, fish residues, fruit wastes, vegetable wastes, waxes — animal and plant.

Pyramid of Numbers The numerical relationship between life forms in different niches *q.v.*

Pyrolysis or destructive distillation. The re-forming of material in an inert atmosphere to produce combustible gases, volatile fluids, tar and charcoal; solid domestic refuse is placed in a retort and heated without additional air to temperatures between 500° C and 1000° C, its weight being reduced by 90 per cent. The solid residue remaining is then disposed of at land-fill *q.v.* sites. Industrial wastes can be reduced by up to 65 per cent in volume. It is a potentially valuable method of obtaining valuable products from used automobile tyres.

Q

Qualitative Analysis An analysis which seeks to determine what components are present in significant amounts in a substance or mixture of substances; such analysis is designed to indicate the presence or absence of specific chemical species, and not their respective quantities.

See Quantitative Analysis.

Quality of Life In current usage, a phrase which appears to cover a miscellany of desirable things not recognized, or not adequately recognized, in the market place. Some qualities of the life of a community which cannot readily be valued or measured include such matters as civil liberties, compassion, justice, freedom, fair play. Secondly, there are such things as health and education, clean air and water, recreation, wild life, enjoyment of wilderness — desirable "goods" which are partly or wholly outside the market economy. The list does not end there, for the individual's life and its quality is strongly influenced by personal and family relationships, community relationships, real income, security of employment, job satisfaction, travelling time, housing conditions, diet and general stress.

See also Conservation, Human Progress Index, Stress.

Quantitative Analysis   An analysis which seeks to determine the relative amounts of significant compounds present in a substance or mixture of substances. There is no sharp demarcation between qualitative and quantitative procedures.
   See Qualitative Analysis.

Quaternary Era   The geological period succeeding the Tertiary Era, and extending to the present time; it is subdivided into Pleistocene and Recent (Holocene) epochs.
   See Geological Time Scale.

R

Rad   The unit of absorbed radiation dose; a dose which results in the absorption of 100 ergs per gram of specified material.
   See Rem.

Radioactive Half-life   *See* Half-Life.

Radioactivity   The spontaneous emission of ionizing particles and rays following the disintegration of certain atomic nuclei. Man is continuously exposed to ionizing radiations from natural sources; radioactive substances are widely distributed in rocks, soils, water and air. Sedimentary rock areas contribute an average dose of about 45 millirems per year, while granite areas such as Aberdeen in Scotland contribute more than double this dose. Higher background levels are to be expected in areas containing deposits of uranium, thorium and radium, perhaps several times as much. Natural gamma radiation directly from the earth and from buildings represents usually about one-half of the total external radiation to which populations are exposed. All food and drinking water contains minute quantities of radium which are ingested into the system; the variations in content depend upon the radioactivity of the rocks and soils from which they are derived. Radon *q.v.* in the atmosphere and cosmic rays also contribute to the general level of radiation.
   The world average dose received from natural and unavoidable background radiation by the individual is

estimated to be about 150 millirems per year. This may vary from between 80 to 300 millirems depending upon the composition of the ground, building materials, altitude, foodstuffs, and so on; the average for the United Kingdom has been estimated to be about 100 millirems per year. Sources of additional radiation to which a person may be exposed include the various forms of radiation used in medicine and industry, the radioactive isotopes

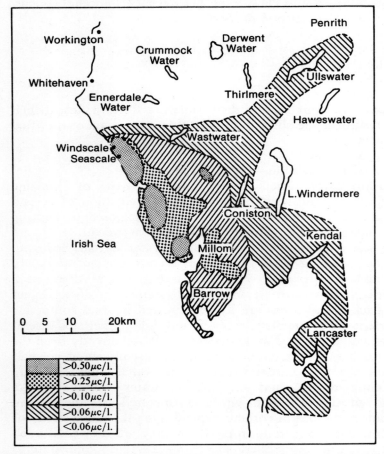

Figure 12   Map of the windscale area showing contours of radio-iodine contamination in milk on 13 October 1957 (Source: Medical Research Council, *The Hazards to Man of Nuclear and Allied Radiation*, Cmnd. 1225, London: H.M.S.O., 1960)

produced in nuclear reactors, accidents in nuclear reactors, and fall-out resulting from the explosion of nuclear weapons. As a result of the Partial Test Ban of 1963, the levels of radioactivity arising from the explosion of nuclear devices have tended to decrease. However, testing by the French authorities on Mururoa Atoll, near Tahiti, of nuclear devices continues to be a source of anxiety.
See Rem. *Also* Figure 12.

Radionuclide Any radioactive nuclide, a nuclide being an atom characterized by the constitution of its nucleus, i.e. by the atomic number and the mass number.

Radiosonde A small radio transmitter carried by a balloon by means of which observations may be obtained from the atmosphere *q.v.* at various heights. Observations are usually of pressure, temperature and humidity.

Radon A radioactive gas that is released from the soil into the atmosphere. It is also released during the combustion of fossil fuel, and for this reason there is more radon in the air over cities than in country air.
See Radioactivity.

Rain Forest A dense, luxuriant, closed, mesomorphic community; a global vegetation type containing many tree species associated with high rainfall and humidity, and a relative absence of frosts. Australia has been particularly well-endowed with rain forests in North Queensland, eastern Australia, and Tasmania; they form a broken band along the coast and adjacent highlands from Cape York to Tasmania; the distribution depends upon altitude, moisture availability, the nature of the soil, the aspect of the slope, the incidence of fire, damage by tropical cyclones and the impact of man.

There are many types of rain forest, though it is usual to consider three major divisions — the tropical, subtropical, and temperate. The preservation of different types of rain forest has become an important issue.

Rainout A process in which particles in the higher troposphere *q.v.* may act as nuclei on which water droplets form, later to fall as rain.

Rebound The elevation of a part of the surface of the earth during or following the removal of overlying material or the filling of an underground cavity.

Receptor   or target. The organism, population, or resource, exposed to specific risks from pollution *q.v.* or other adverse influences.

Recycling   The return of discarded or waste materials to the production system for utilization in the manufacture of goods, with a view to the conservation as far as practicable of non-renewable and scarce resources. Recycling goes beyond the re-use of a product (such as glass milk bottles) and involves the return of salvaged materials, such as paper or metals or broken glass, to an early stage (pulping or melting stage) of the manufacturing process. Some recycling has always been profitable to certain industries (e.g. the return of steel scrap to the steel industry); opinion now seems to favour an increased tempo and scale of recycling to conserve resources for the future of mankind beyond what may be profitable in the shorter term. The capacity of an industry to recycle is in many cases limited by technical as well as economic considerations. On the other hand, the glass industry is already recycling considerable quantities of cullett and appears able and willing to accept more. The aluminium industry currently finds it economically acceptable to encourage the return of aluminium drink cans.

See Non-Renewable Resources.

Red-tide   or red-sea. Descriptive effect of the red-brown colour of dense populations of marine protozoa *q.v.* which can occur under exceptionally favourable conditions of water temperature, salinity, and/or nutrient salts. The accumulation of metabolic wastes in these conditions may cause massive fish mortality.

Reducer   In biology, a heterotrophic individual which utilizes the chemical energy of organic matter while breaking it down or reducing it to more simple substances.

Refuse   The complete range of unwanted or undesirable material generated in the course of producing, processing and consuming useful products.

See Composting, Compression, Land-Fill.

Relative Biological Effectiveness   The ratio of the dose (in rads) of gamma radiation from cobalt-60 to the dose (in rads) of any type of ionizing radiation which produces the same, specified, biological effect.

See Rad.

Relative Humidity The ratio between the actual weight of water vapour in a given volume of air and the amount which would be present if the air was saturated at the same temperature, expressed as a percentage.

Rem Abbreviation for "roentgen equivalent man"; a unit of dose of ionizing radiation. The quantity of ionizing radiation which has the same specified biological effect as one rad *q.v.* of gamma radiation *q.v.* from cobalt-60.

Reservation The withholding from use and exploitation of areas and resources which it is judged should be held back either against future needs or because they are best kept as they are; areas so treated are called 'reserves', e.g. forest reserves or game reserves.

Residual A quantity of material or energy which is left over or "wasted" when, in the course of human activity, inputs are converted into outputs in production and consumption. Examples are waste-heat and gaseous pollutants from thermal-electricity generation, slag from metal ore refining. Outputs have prices in normally existing markets; residuals do not. Through a change in economic circumstances or technological advance, a residual may become an output. Scrap metal or glass recovery at a refuse plant converts a waste into an output.
See also Re-Cycling.

Residual Chlorine (Chorine Residual) The amount of available chlorine present in industrial water at any given time after chlorine or hypochlorite has been added to it.
See Chlorination.

Residual Use A use other than a beneficial use *q.v.* in respect of water, e.g. the disposal of liquid effluents.

Resource Management The introduction and enforcement of restraints, including specified technical practices, to safeguard the future of renewable resources and uphold the principle of sustained yield.
See Sustained Yield Conservation.

Rill A small stream, rivulet; in soil erosion *q.v.* rills appear in the top soil.

Riparian Living or situated on the bank of a water-course, such as a river or stream; hence the terms "riparian owner" and "riparian interests".

Riprap A wall of broken rock thrown together irregularly so as to protect embankments from erosion; also used of the rock itself.

Risk   The expected frequency of undesirable effects arising from a given exposure to a pollutant.

River Thames Clean-up   A programme inaugurated in the 1960s to effect an improvement in the quality of the River Thames, London, in its lower reaches.

The Committee on "Pollution of the Tidal Thames" (the Pippard Committee) reported in 1961 that the Thames estuary down to Gravesend was in a badly polluted and frequently offensive state. Hydrogen sulphide was evolved through the activity of sulphate-reducing bacteria when the water was completely de-oxygenated. The Water Pollution Research Laboratory had co-operated with the Committee in investigating these conditions. It was found that the sewage works at Barking and Crossness, Mogden, Acton and Dartford were responsible for about nine-tenths of the sewage effluent discharged into the tidal Thames, the Barking and Crossness works together contributing roughly half the polluting load from all sources. The direct discharge from Acton, while comparatively small, was also found to be a significant source of pollution.

Stormwater discharges, so far as could be estimated, contributed about 1½ per cent of the total pollution entering the estuary, but as these discharges entered further upstream than the largest sewage discharges they had a greater effect than suggested by the percentage figure.

Direct industrial discharges accounted for about 3 per cent of the total polluting load. Sulphide discharged from the sulphur dioxide scrubbing plant at the Battersea and Bankside power stations, while it had no material effect on the rest of the estuary, caused an appreciable loss of oxygen from the river water near the power station. The Report recommended that the aeration of discharges should be increased.

While the Upper Thames and the tributaries contributed dissolved oxygen and nitrate to the estuary, they were found to contribute polluting matter also. Of the tributaries, the Wandle was found to have the greatest polluting effect. It was found that the introduction of synthetic detergents in and after 1949 was followed by a marked lengthening of the zone devoid of oxygen.

Heated effluents from power stations had caused increases of up to 5 degrees Celsius in the temperature of the estuary. In the presence of available oxygen, the effect of these discharges was to accelerate the loss of oxygen locally. When there was no available oxygen and sulphate was being reduced to sulphide, these heated discharges would accelerate the evolution of hydrogen sulphide. The Report recommended the aeration of power station effluents in order to increase the oxygen content.

The Committee also recommended the pursuit of measures to prevent offensive conditions and the creation of a "margin of safety". It was noted, however, that to raise the dissolved oxygen enough for salmon to pass through the estuary would require extremely high standards of effluent purity, and imply an expense out of proportion to any likely gain. The Committee recommended that new polluting discharges to the estuary above Lower Hope Reach should be avoided if at all possible; even below this point, proposals for new discharges should be carefully considered. The Committee thought that the imposition of uniform standards of quality was not suitable save for minor effluents; standards for effluents must control the quantity of polluting matter discharged hence the volume as well as the strength of each effluent must be known.

There can be no doubt that improvements at sewage works and in the treatment of other effluents has led to a marked improvement in the condition of the Thames. By 1969, the sand goby, flounder and smelt were being found on the screens at Fulham power station which is situated 16 kilometres above London Bridge and 64 kilometres from the sea. Other fish found at Fulham have included eel, pike, bream, roach, perch and trout; salmon have yet to return. Undoubtedly, the Thames has not been cleaner for more than a century.

Rough Fish   Fish undesirable as game or food. Most destructive of all rough fish is the carp; it may uproot extensive quantities of vegetation during foraging activities and cause muddied waters.

Royal Commission Standards Standards for the quality of sewage works effluents recommended by a Royal Commission on Sewage Disposal which was appointed in Britain in 1898 to report on the methods available for the treatment and disposal of sewage and trade wastes. The Commission recommended standards for sewage effluents discharging to inland streams (other than storm water sewage). The type of treatment envisaged was sedimentation and complete biological treatment, and the standards were a maximum biochemical oxygen demand (BOD) of not more than 20 g/m^3 and a maximum concentration of suspended solids of not more than 30 g/m^3, by weight, where the dilution factor was not less than 8:1. The Commission also suggested a limiting concentration of 40 to 60 g/m^3 of suspended solids for trade effluents discharging into inland streams, the exact value depending on the nature of the effluent. The aim of the standards was to avoid nuisance. These standards are still considered fairly good today, although an increasing number of situations demand more exacting standards and hence tertiary treatment *q.v.*

Run-off The discharge of water through surface streams into larger watercourses.

S

Salinity The total content of dissolved mineral constituents, of all kinds, in water. Normally the problem of excessive salinity in rivers does not arise. Rain and other forms of precipitation are relatively free of minerals; it is when these waters come into contact with the earth that the process of mineralization begins. Natural sources of salinity include springs passing through rock formations which contain soluble salts. Other sources of salinity include domestic and industrial wastes, oil-well brines, and mine water. The use and re-use of water, particularly where irrigation is carried out, increases the threat of excessive salinity which makes water unsuitable for public supply and for further irrigation. Water containing more than 500 ppm of dissolved solids is not considered desirable for domestic supplies. Water containing more than about 2,000 ppm is considered to be unsuitable for irrigation under average conditions, in the long term. High levels of salinity in soil water in Australia are a major environmental hazard associated with agriculture, and particularly with irrigation. In many areas the groundwater *q.v.* is naturally saline. The clearing of natural vegetation on land in southern Australia for agriculture and replacement with introduced grasses has brought, through reduced evapotranspiration *q.v.,* a rise in the water-table *q.v.* In consequence, in a number of localities, considerable areas have gone out of production.

Average salinities in Australian rivers are generally less than 400 g/m^3 of total dissolved solids; a major exception is the Murray, the largest river system in Australia, where salinity may reach 800 g/m^3 in the lower reaches, depending on the dryness of the season. Factors contributing to this salinity include flows from tributary catchments, ground water inflow, surface drainage, and subsurface drain effluents from irrigated areas. The salinity problem of the Murray is particularly important because of the number of agricultural and urban users who are supplied from it.

Sand Mining Refers usually to the extraction of the natural concentrations of heavy minerals contained in some parts of the vast mass of marine sands which mantle the eastern seaboard of Australia. Rutile and zircon constitute much of this heavy mineral fraction. Conflict has arisen between sand mining and beneficial uses in respect of Fraser Island, Cooloola, Moreton Island and Stradbroke Island in Queensland; the Myall Lakes in New South Wales; and the Blackwood River in Western Australia.

See also Coastal Protection.

Sanitary Land-fill *See* Land-Fill.

Santa Barbara "Blow-out" An incident which occurred on 28 January 1969, while the Union Oil Company was drilling its fourth well from an offshore rig located about 13 kilometres from the shore of the Santa Barbara Channel, off the coast of California. Pressure in the hole rose suddenly, blew out all the drilling mud, and crude oil spurted from the ocean floor. The blow-out continued for ten days. The first slick of oil reached Rincon, 24 kilometres from the drilling platform, some five days after the blow-out; three days later it arrived at Santa Barbara, surging on to the beaches, promenades, and jetties. Seagulls avoided the oil, but many grebes dived into it and died slowly. Santa Barbara was a declared a Federal disaster area. The Union Oil Company spent close on $5 million making good the damage, collecting blackened birds, washing and caring for them. Dispersives were sprayed on the oil. Tons of straw were blasted at high pressure on to water, beaches, rocks and docks, functioning as "blotting paper". The straw was later collected and removed. Blackened sand was removed from the beaches. The oil well was sealed with mud and cement, but cracks continued to occur in the ocean floor around the platform causing seepage; special measures were adopted to deal with this seepage.

See Oil Pollution.

Saprophyte   A plant which lives on decaying organic matter; most saprophites are fungi.

Sea-Breeze   The movement of air from sea to land. On clear days the land usually heats faster than water. The lowest air layer adjacent to the land warms quickly; this is displaced by inflowing heavier and cooler sea air.

See Land-Breeze.

Sea-Salt   An important natural air pollutant which adds to the general corrosiveness of the atmosphere, particularly in maritime countries such as Britain.

Sea-Water Distillation   A purification process involving the evaporation of sea-water and subsequent condensation of the vapour; the undesirable suspended and dissolved solids remain in the residue.

Secondary Treatment   A series of biochemical, chemical and mechanical processes used in sewage treatment *q.v.*, which remove, oxidize, or stabilize non-settleable, colloidal, and dissolved organic materials found in sewage, following primary treatment. The two techniques most commonly used are either treatment on trickling filters or the activated sludge process *q.v.* These carry out in a controlled manner the biological assimilation and degradation processes that occur in nature. Trickling filters *q.v.*, also known as biological filters, consist of beds of coarse material over which the sewage is sprinkled at a uniform rate; they are generally not less than two metres deep and circular in plan. The activated sludge process of sewage treatment is in effect an artificially accelerated self-purification process, promoted by oxidation. As in the case of the trickling filter, the impurities in the sewage are oxidized mainly by the action of aerobic bacteria. The most common method of introducing oxygen into the sewage in the activated sludge process is to blow compressed air through porous plates placed in the bottom of the tanks; under-water paddles assist in the distribution of air and help to keep the sludge in suspension. The sewage, after passing through the activated sludge tanks, is allowed to settle in secondary sedimentation tanks; after a suitable detention time the activated sludge (other than that mixed with fresh sewage) is pumped to sludge digestion chambers.

Sedimentary Cycle The circulation of nutrients in an eco-system *q.v.* involving geological weathering and erosion with the eventual recovery of the elements by the uplift of marine sediments to form land masses.

Sedimentary Rock Rock formed by the accumulation of material derived from rock fragments or the remains of animals or plants; also products of chemical action.
See also Igneous Rock, Metamorphic Rock.

Sedimentation The removal of settleable solids within primary or secondary treatment plants using settling tanks; the low velocity of the sewage flowing through the system allows particles to gravitate to the bottom, permitting ready removal as sludge.
See Sewage Treatment.

Seepage Pit A buried perforated tank or gravel-filled cavity allowing effluent, e.g. from a septic tank, to seep into the surrounding soil.

Self-cleansing The general tendency of a body of air to recover naturally from contamination by waste gases. Pollution *q.v.* in many forms is continually being intro-duced into the atmosphere *q.v.* If the atmosphere did not have certain self-cleansing powers its condition would quickly become intolerable. Particles of sufficient size are removed from the atmosphere by gravitation Smaller particles (say $< 20 \mu m$) may be removed from the atmosphere by impaction on the surface of the earth or vegetation or on buildings. Rainfall also plays a part in collecting and removing particles; gaseous contaminants may be absorbed in rain and fog. The character of pollutants may be modified by photochemical or chemical reactions which may accelerate or retard the effect of pollutants on man, animal or vegetation. The "balance" is much affected by the meteorological factors and topography of the city or town under consideration. Some localities are normally poorly-ventilated with a resultant aggravation of their pollution problems. Others are well-ventilated and can dispose of more pollutants by dispersion into the atmosphere for a comparable level of pollution. The frequency, intensity and duration of temperature inversions in the atmosphere (when the temperature of the atmosphere increases instead of falling with height which has the effect of inhibiting the upward diffusion of gases) is a major factor influencing the dispersal of pollutants.

The atmosphere is a dynamic system. It steadily absorbs and relinquishes a range of solid, liquid and gaseous pollutants from both natural and man-made sources. While being dispersed through the effects of turbulence, some of these pollutants will react between themselves and with other substances, both chemically and physically, yielding a variety of other compounds. Whether or not in their original form some of these pollutants will eventually reach a sink (such as the ocean) or a receptor (such as man or vegetation). The description "self-cleansing" appears to have been attached to bodies of air, while the equivalent expression "self-purification", has been used of bodies of water.

Self-Purification   The general tendency of a body of water to recover naturally from contamination by organic wastes; thus when a river receives, continuously or intermittently, quantities of organic wastes it will tend to purify itself and recover naturally in the course of time. This process of self-purification depends very largely upon biochemical reactions in which bacteria (and other micro-organisms) in the presence of sufficient dissolved oxygen use the organic matter as food, breaking down complex compounds into simpler and relatively harmless products. Other factors such as dilution, sedimentation and sunlight also play an important part in the self-purification process. However, the dominant requirement is a sufficient quantity of dissolved oxygen. If this is used up, that is the rate of absorption of oxygen exceeds the rate of replenishment, self-purification will cease and a septic condition will prevail. Septic conditions are associated with offensive odours, floating masses of black sludge and the termination of aquatic life.

The oxidation of organic matter during self-purification is effected in two stages:

1. Carbonaceous oxidation stage, in which most of the organic carbon is oxidized to carbon dioxide. Water and ammonia are also formed from the hydrogen and nitrogen of organic matter.
2. Nitrification stage, in which biochemical oxidation of ammonia to nitrous and ultimately nitric acid occurs, and the residual organic carbon is consumed.

Finally, a dark brown or almost black complex organic material remains, known as humus *q.v.* Deposited by the river-bed, it is very resistent to further decomposition by micro-organisms. Humus contains carbon, hydrogen, oxygen and nitrogen with a C:N ratio of about 10:1 . A shallow, fast-flowing watercourse will purify itself in a much shorter period of time than a watercourse which is deep and sluggish, through a higher rate of re-aeration. The speed of chemical or biochemical reactions increases with a rise in temperature; hence the process of self purification will tend to be more rapid in the summer months than in the winter months. The speeding up of the process will increase the amount of dissolved oxygen required in any given length of river or stream. However, since warm water contains much less dissolved oxygen than cold water, a heavy pollution load has a greater likelihood of de-oxygenating a river or stream in the summer than in the winter, thereby creating septic conditions. In addition, lower summer rainfalls may result in lower dilution factors.

Separate System   A drainage system in which foul sewage and surface-water are conveyed in separate pipes.

Septic   A biochemical condition depending on anaerobic bacterial activity, characterized by putrefaction.

Septic Tank   A watertight sedimentation tank for organic wastes in which the sludge settling on the bottom is allowed to digest and liquefy by anaerobic bacterial action. The tank may be emptied at intervals by a special vehicle, or the effluent may pass into a seepage tank or system of agricultural pipes for final absorption into suitable ground. If an all-wastes septic tank is combined with a sand filter and a chlorination unit, it resembles a miniature sewage works capable, with good maintenance, of handling the wastes from an individual premise or small group of premises.

Sessile   Permanently attached; stationary; or on a base without a stalk.

Sewage   The contents of sewers carrying the waterborne wastes of a community. Sometimes the term "foul sewage" is used to distinguish between sewage, as defined here, and the contents of sewers carrying surface or storm water only.

Sewage Farming   Sewage farming, an alternative method of sewage treatment *q.v.*, is in effect the use of sewage for irrigation. It is a method which may be employed in areas of low rainfall. This method of treatment may be seen in Melbourne, Australia, where the sewage from practically the entire city has been treated at a sewage farm at Werribee, about thirty kilometres from the city centre. The Werribee farm has served nearly two million people; 520,000 cubic metres per day of sewage has been disposed of to 108 square kilometres of land. The precise procedure used (land filtration, grass filtration, or lagooning) has depended on the season. While the nutrient load has been reduced by about 50 per cent, the run-off passes into Port Phillip Bay contributing a significant nutrient load. The existing sewage treatment facilities have been overloaded, but there will be adequate alternative and additional treatment facilities during the latter part of the decade when the Southeastern Purification Plant at Carrum comes into operation.

Sewage Fungus Unsightly slimes resulting sometimes from the pollution of rivers by discharges of organic matter.

Sewage Treatment The modification of sewage to make it more acceptable to the environment. Sewage treatment may be divided into four main stages:

1. Primary Treatment The removal of suspended matter by physical and mechanical means, e.g., screening, grinding, flocculation or sedimentation.
2. Secondary Treatment The removal of finely suspended solids and colloidal matter, and the stabilization and oxidation of these substances and the dissolved organic matter by means of air and the activity of living organisms.
3. Tertiary Treatment The attainment of higher effluent standards for many purposes.
4. Sludge Disposal The disposal of the suspended matter removed.

A decision as to the stages of treatment to be adopted depends on what is to become of the final effluent. A town situated close to the sea may discharge its sewage without pre-treatment at a suitable distance out to sea; this approach is known as disposal by dilution. Where conditions are not satisfactory for this method of disposal, pre-treatment becomes necessary. With regard to inland towns, the final effluent which will be discharged into a watercourse undergoes at least two stages of treatment.

See Primary Treatment, Secondary Treatment, Sludge Digestion, Tertiary Treatment.

Sewerage A physical arrangement of pipes and plant for the collection, removal, treatment, and disposal of liquid wastes.

Shadow Price A price or value imputed to unpriced social benefits or losses or to resources which are not satisfactorily priced in commercial markets. The concept is much used in cost-benefit analysis. In evaluating any project, the economist may adjust a number of market prices and attribute prices to unpriced gains and losses likely to arise.

See Polluter Pays Principle.

Shelter Belt Belts of trees purposely planted to provide protection against prevailing winds; soil erosion *q.v.* is retarded by this technique and crop yields generally improved.

Shifting Cultivation *See* Swidden Agriculture.

Silt An unconsolidated sediment of inorganic granular material which has been transported mechanically and deposited; in size the particles are between sands and clays.

Slow Sand Filter A shallow basin, partly filled with sand and provided with an under-drainage system which is used for the purification of surface-waters intended for domestic water supplies.

Sludge Cake The residue left on the filter after the filtration of a sludge.

Sludge Digestion A final biochemical reduction stage in sewage treatment *q.v.* Raw sludge is a semi-liquid whose solids content varies with the source which may be primary sedimentation, trickling filter *q.v.* or activated sludge process *q.v.* The primary purpose of sludge digestion is to change the offensive fresh sludge into an innocuous residue, the organic matter in the fresh sludge being broken down and stabilized by bacteria and other micro-organisms. Digestion of sludge also results in a reduction in volume and improved ability to drain and dry. The products of digestion are withdrawn as gas, supernatant liquor and digested sludge. The proceeds from the sale of sludge, if any, help to reduce the overall cost of processing.

The factors having the greatest influence on the rate of digestion are temperature and acidity. To achieve the best results the temperature is maintained at not less than 27°C and the sludge should always be slightly alkaline. In colder climates artificial heating of the sludge is necessary. In the process of sludge digestion the heavier solids separate from the liquid and settle to the bottom whilst floating solids rise to the surface to form scum. The space between the two layers of solids is occupied by a liquid known as "supernatant liquor". In most treatment plants the supernatant liquor is drawn off and returned to the primary settling tank.

Properly-digested sludge is blackish in colour, containing up to 95 per cent water. To remove the water the sludge is spread on drained sand-drying beds. Mechanical methods of dewatering sludges are being increasingly considered as alternatives to drying beds; they occupy less site space and are not subject to the vagaries of the weather.

Dried Sludge can be used as filling or as a soil builder; it possesses some fertility value. Considerable research effort is being devoted to work on the treatment and disposal of sludges, as this process frequently involves greater difficulties than any other waste-treatment operation. Sludge disposal may account for about 25 to 50 per cent of the capital and operating costs of treatment. It is not, however, directly connected with water pollution unless allowed to enter a stream or other body of water.

Sometimes the final sewage effluent may be disinfected by chlorination. To ensure an effective destruction of 99.9 per cent of the sewage bacteria it is necessary to have a chlorine residual of 0.2 to 0.4 parts per million after 20 to 30 minutes of contact.

Smog A term first used by the late Dr. H. A. Voeux, founder-president of the British National Smoke Abatement Society in 1905 to denote a combination of smoke and natural fog which, in urban areas, may have unpleasant and even disastrous consequences. This handy journalistic expression is in use now in all countries, although in some areas such as California it refers to a kind of air pollution which is of a vastly different character, e.g. Los Angeles smog *q.v.* is of photochemical origin, containing neither smoke nor fog.

See Air Pollution.

Smoke A common carbonaceous contaminant of town air; the visible products of incomplete combustion. Smoke is undesirable for several reasons:

1. As visible evidence of incomplete combustion it involves a significant waste of fuel
2. In fouling boiler heating surfaces, it reduces the heat transfer rate, increases fuel consumption and maintenance costs
3. Being dirty and perhaps greasy it possesses a high soiling capacity
4. It contains substances suspected of being carcinogenic to man
5. It obscures sunlight, generates murk and gloom, and

increases the intensity and duration of fogs.

In addition to carbon, tar and ash, droplets containing dissolved salts and sulphuric acid have been recognized as common constituents of urban air. The vast majority of smoke particles are much less than 1 μm in size and may only be examined in any detail by an electron microscope; the particles may sometimes form chains up to 1 μm in length.

The British Committee on Air Pollution accepted the view that, with few exceptions, no industrial chimney need normally emit more than a light haze of smoke if the combustion arrangements are adequate and properly operated. The exceptions which the Committee had in mind included:

1. The emission of dark smoke for occasional short periods when fires are being lighted, or raked, or during soot-blowing, or in cases of mechanical breakdown
2. The emission of dark smoke from industrial processes in which, according to present knowledge, the prevention of dark smoke entails special technical difficulties, e.g., the manufacture of Staffordshire blue engineering bricks.

Industrial steam-raising plant does not present "special technical difficulties" and smoke can be avoided by the promotion of efficient combustion. Efficient combustion depends upon:

1. A sufficient supply of air (oxygen) in relation to the amount of fuel to be burned
2. An intimate mixing of fuel and air to ensure that every particle of fuel or molecule of volatile gas receives a sufficient amount of air
3. An adequate temperature not only to initiate combustion but to sustain it
4. A sufficient amount of time to allow combustion to be completed before any combustible gases impinge on cool, flame-quenching surfaces.

In practice an excess of air is necessary over the theoretical amount required to achieve intimate mixing. Given sufficient air, efficient combustion then depends on time, temperature and turbulence (the three Ts).

See also Air Pollution.

Social Rank The order of individuals within a community or population *q.v.* in a dominance hierarchy.

Sociosphere The area of study of the social scientist; analogous to the hydrosphere as the area of study of the oceanographer, the biosphere as the area of study of the biologist, and the lithosphere as the area of study of the geologist. The sociosphere embraces people, their roles and patterns of behaviour, their organizations and groups, and social interactions.

Sodium Fluoracetate ('1080') A rodenticide marketed under the designation '1080'; it is manufactured from ethyl chloroacetate and potassium fluoride which react to give ethyl fluoracetate; this is then hydrolysed with sodium hydroxide in methyl-alcohol. Highly toxic, sodium fluoracetate is very stable. Its toxicity for rabbits is very high, and indeed is one of the main tools of rabbit control in Australia. It is normally distributed in oats or chopped carrot. Strict regulations govern its use.

Soil The loose material which forms the upper layer of the mantle rock of the Earth, consisting mainly of very small particles of inorganic mineral matter plus humus *q.v.*; the depth of soil varies up to several metres and is the material from which roots derive both food and moisture. The 'top soil' is the soil that is cultivated; it is more fertile and contains more organic matter than the subsoil which lies beneath it. Soil creep is the almost imperceptible but continuous movement of surface soil down slopes, under the influence of thermal and precipitation effects.
See also Soil Conservation, Soil Erosion, Laterite.

Soil Conservation The devising and implementing of systems of land-use *q.v.* and management so that there will be no loss of stability, productivity, or usefulness of the soil *q.v.* in relation to the selected purpose. The soils of Australia are old, heavily leached and, in general, relatively shallow. In 1971, a special report of the Commonwealth Standing Committee on Soil Conservation revealed that approximately one-third of the non-arid area of Australia was affected to some degree by soil erosion and, of that portion, one-third was regarded as being affected by major erosion. Control of soil erosion is a State responsibility and all States have implemented soil conservation programmes aimed at repairing the structural damage which has occurred already and at the development of policies for improved systems of land use to prevent further deterioration. There is, however, a serious continuing problem of loss of productive land due to soil erosion *q.v.*

Conservation tillage practices have been introduced to the Darling Downs in Southeast Queensland. The tillage practices involved are mainly stubble mulching and minimum tillage — these represent some of the most important soil conservation measures in the grain-growing areas of Queensland. The adoption of these practices contributes greatly to the re-instatement of natural hydrologic and hydraulic regimes, and consequently reduces soil erosion rates.

Soil Erosion   The loss of soil *q.v.* as a result of natural and human activities. Natural erosion is the starting point of pedogenesis (creation of soils) which is indispensable to sustain human life; on the other hand, accelerated erosion due to bad soil management, deforestation *q.v.*, brush and forest fires, overgrazing and poor agricultural practices destroys the soil, with far-reaching consequences. Among the most important measures for combating soil erosion are re-afforestation, reduction of overgrazing, return of manure to the land, terracing of mountain slopes and contour ploughing.

Soil Erosion Control   *See* Contour Farming, Contour Strip Cropping, Gully Reclamation, Shelter Belts, Terracing.

Solar Energy   The energy of the sun which reaches the Earth in the form of short-wave radiation, visible light and near-ultra-violet light. After penetrating the atmosphere *q.v.*, part of the energy heats the surface of the Earth and part of it is re-radiated back in the form of long-wave radiation and absorbed by water vapour and carbon dioxide in the atmosphere. The latter radiates again about half of the captured energy back towards the Earth's surface. The warming caused by the trapped energy has been called a greenhouse effect *q.v.* The possible utilization of solar energy for the generation of electricity is receiving an increasing amount of attention in Australia and elsewhere where sunlight is abundant. While sunlight is essential to living things, it is thought, in Australia, to be the most frequent cause of skin cancer.

Solid Waste Management A planned system of effectively controlling the production, storage, collection, transportation, processing and disposal or utilization of solid wastes in a sanitary, aesthetically acceptable, and economical manner. It includes all administrative, financial, legal, and planning functions, as well as the physical aspects of solid waste handling.

Solid Wastes All material of a solid or semi-solid character that the possessor no longer considers of sufficient value to retain.

Sonic Boom or supersonic bang. Caused by supersonic aircraft "crashing the sound barrier", i.e. flying faster than the velocity of sound (about 1,200 kilometres per hour).

Sound Wave The result of pressure variations in the air caused by a series of compressions and rarefactions moving outwards from some vibrating object. The frequency of the sound wave is the rate at which successive pressure variations reach the eardrum. Each wave − first a compression then a rarefaction − on encountering an object, exerts a force; this is why sound can break a glass or vibrate a window. Frequency is expressed as the number of vibrations per second or cycles per second (1 cycle per second = 1 hertz (Hz)); the frequency of a wave is also the number of complete waves that pass a given point in one second.

Source Control The elimination, before or during the consumption of a product, of potential air contaminants contained in raw materials, thus preventing the emission of contaminants to the atmosphere.

  See Air Pollution.

Spaceship Earth An expression coined, probably independently, by Professor Kenneth E. Boulding and Barbara Ward (Lady Jackson) which appeared in separate works published in 1966; it conveys a view of the Earth from space, dramatizing the image of man as inhabiting a small, closed spaceship, with destination unknown and resources limited.

Space-time Continuum The four-dimensional continuum of the real world, utilizing three dimensions of space and one of time. A static-state description of a system utilized only space dimensions at any one time: a dynamic description utilizes all four dimensions, being a succession of static-state descriptions through time.

Species A group whose members have a close mutual resemblance, having a common origin and a continuous breeding system; the smallest unit of classification commonly used. The members of a species form a reproductively isolatedgroup.

See Sub-Species.

Speed of Sound The speed at which a sound pulse travels, being 334 metres per second in air at 20° C.

—Sphere *See* Atmosphere, Biosphere, Ecosphere, Geosphere, Hydrosphere, Ionosphere, Lithosphere, Ozonosphere, Sociosphere, Stratosphere, Troposphere.

Standard Levels of exposure to pollutants which should not be exceeded; standards may be statutory or presumptive. Two levels have been adopted by the U.S. Environmental Protection Agency.

1. Primary. Levels judged necessary to protect health with an adequate margin of safety

2. Secondary. Levels judged necessary to protect public welfare from any known or anticipated adverse effects.

These are essentially environmental quality standards. Standards may also prescribe the contents of products, e.g. the amount of phosphates in detergents, or pesticide residues in foodstuffs. They may also take the form of emission standards, e.g. the upper limits of what may be emitted from the exhausts of motor vehicles or from the chimneys of industrial plants.

See Product Standard.

Standing Crop The biomass *q.v.* or organic matter present on a given area at a given time; it usually varies in quantity with the season.

Star Town A form of town development to deal with growth and contain urban sprawl; compact satellite towns are developed within easy access of the main town centre and in a peripheral ring around it.

Static Stability A fundamental concept inmeteorology *q.v.,* it refers to what happens to a parcel of air after it has been given an initial vertical displacement, either upwards or downwards. If, after an upward displacement, the parcel is found to be warmer (less dense) than its surroundings, its buoyancy will make it move farther from its original position; it will continue to move until its temperature (and density) become equal to that of its surroundings. In this instance in which a parcel moves farther from its original level, the surrounding atmosphere *q.v.* is said to be statically unstable (or just unstable). If after displacement, however, the parcel is found to be colder (more dense) than its surroundings, its buoyancy will tend to return the parcel to its original level; the surrounding atmosphere is then said to be statically stable (or just stable). In the intermediate stage when the vertical motion is neither encouraged nor opposed the atmosphere is said to be neutrally stable. The concept of static stability is of considerable importance in the study of the dispersal of air pollutants in the atmosphere.

See Air Pollution.

Steepness of Slope A characteristic of land expressed in terms of percentages, e.g. a 10 per cent slope is one which drops 10 metres over a horizontal distance of 100 metres. Intensity of water run-off *q.v.* and soil erosion *q.v.* are partially dependent on the relative slope of the terrain.

Stenohaline Unable to endure wide variation of osmotic pressure of environment, e.g. wide variation in the salinity of water. Opposite of euryhaline.

Storm Tank A tank, usually located at a sewage treatment *q.v.* works, provided for storage and partial treatment of excess storm sewage prior to discharge to a watercourse or other body of water.

Storm Sewage Foul sewage mixed with relatively large quantities of surface-water.

Storm Water Natural water from the surface of the ground, paved areas and roofs.

Storm Water Overflow An arrangement whereby all excess flow of sewage and surface-water in a combined sewer system is by-passed to a watercourse. A common engineering practice has been to provide for the interception and treatment of a sewage and surface-water flow equal to two or three times the average dry-weather flow; all flow in excess of this amount is directed to a water course. Storm water overflows may be provided at several points in a system. Of major concern during periods of overflow or surcharge are the flooding of basements with a mixture of sewage and storm water, and the additional pollution load imposed on watercourses It is not feasible to design systems which will accept the maximum possible flow, due to the large volumes of run-off which occur in very short periods of time. One solution is to completely separate the sewage and surface-water systems, so that no storm water enters the sewage system; another lies in the provision of holding tanks or ponds to receive excess storm water and release it slowly to treatment plants or water-courses.

Stratosphere The upper layer of the atmosphere lying above the troposphere *q.v.* (above about 11 kilometres altitude) in which the temperature remains constant with height.

Streamflow Regulation A method of water quality control in which good quality stored water, is added to a stream at times of deteriorating stream water quality. There are three parts to an effective streamflow regulation scheme:
1. the deterioration of downstream water quality must be determinable
2. good quality, impounded water must be available for release and must be released as required
3. there must be a beneficial effect downstream from the release of impounded water.

See Beneficial Use, Water Pollution.

Stress The non-specific response of a body or organism to any demand made upon it, primarily preparing the organism for physical activity, e.g. fight or flight. Stress is one of the mechanisms suspected of leading to disease in modern life.

See Psychosocial Stressors.

Structural Conservation That aspect of conservation *q.v.* concerned with works or practices aimed at improved management of the environment, e.g. soil and water conservation measures, coastal defence works, land reclamation measures, flood control.

Sublimation The passage of water vapour directly into the solid state, by-passing the liquid state.

Subsidence Inversion A temperature inversion *q.v.* formed in the atmosphere *q.v.* usually well above the earth's surface, as a result of the slow descent of air which becomes warmer through adiabatic compression.

Subsoil Water or ground-water *q.v.* Water occurring naturally in the subsoil.

Sub-species A segment or subdivision of a species *q.v.*, being a group whose members resemble each other in certain characteristics but whose range of variation represents only a portion of the total variation of the species. There may be no sharp dividing line, however, between the various sub-species of the same species.

Substitution Effects The environmental consequences of substituting, for example, one form of control or method of disposal for another. Scrubbing waste gases converts an air pollution *q.v.* problem into a liquid waste problem, while the installation of domestic garbage disposal units converts a solid waste disposal problem into a liquid waste disposal problem.

Succession The replacement of one community *q.v.* or population *q.v.* by another as a result of changes in the environment *q.v.*

Sullage Water Household liquid waste, other than sewage; contaminated water from kitchens, bathrooms and laundries. In unsewered areas, sullage water is often discharged directly to creeks.

See also Combined Sewer, Septic Tank.

Sulphur A non-metallic element occurring in nature in the free state and combined as sulphides and sulphates. It is present in coal and oil, being derived from the substances from which they were formed. The sulphur may be either chemically or physically mixed with the fuel. The sulphur content of coals ranges from 0.3 to 3.5 per cent. Sulphur is present in coal in three forms:
1. pyrites
2. organic sulphur compounds, cleaning processes having virtually no effect on this type of sulphur
3. sulphates, present only in very small quantities and rarely exceeding 0.03 per cent.

The ratio of pyritic to organic sulphur varies considerably. High-rank coals tend to be low in sulphur, medium-rank coals high in sulphur, while low-rank coals appear to be fairly average. During the combustion of coal, most of the sulphur is released to the atmosphere, mainly as sulphur dioxide *q.v.* together with a small amount (3 to 5 per cent) of sulphur trioxide *q.v.* With coal and coke burned in domestic heating appliances, about 20 per cent of the sulphur is retained in the ash or clinker. In industrial boilers and furnaces, only about 10 per cent of the sulphur is retained in the ash. The crude oils of the Middle East have an average sulphur content of about 2.5 per cent; most of this sulphur appears in the final products, being less than 1 per cent in diesel and gas oils and up to 4 per cent or more in residual oils. During the combustion of oil virtually the whole of the sulphur is released to atmosphere, mainly as sulphur dioxide. Australia is fortunate in having access to low-sulphur coals and oil crudes.

Sulphur Cycle   The circulation of sulphur atoms brought about mainly by living things. The decomposition of proteins containing sulphur (e.g. egg albumin) under aerobic conditions results in the formation of sulphates which are odourless and relatively harmless. However, when such proteins undergo decomposition by anaerobic bacteria the foul-smelling gas hydrogen sulphide *q.v.* is produced. Other malodorous sulphur compounds may also be produced under certain conditions, e.g. methyl mercaptan (CH_3SH) will be produced when a river or other body of water is devoid both of dissolved oxygen and nitrate. Sulphur circulates globally between air, land, and sea. A large part of the sulphur in the global atmosphere (as distinct from the atmosphere of towns) is emitted originally as hydrogen sulphide from natural sources; much of this hydrogen sulphide is converted later to sulphur dioxide *q.v.* Sulphur, either in the form of sulphur dioxide, sulphur trioxide *q.v.*, hydrogen sulphide or sulphate salts, is removed from the atmosphere *q.v.* in rain, drizzle and fog, and by gaseous absorption in the oceans. Only about one-third of the discharge to atmosphere is due to combustion processes, the balance being attributable mainly to release from sea-spray and biological decay.

See Biogeochemical Cycles.

Sulphur Dioxide   A colourless, pungent gas formed when sulphur *q.v.* burns in air. It is considered to be one of the most important air pollutants; most of the sulphur dioxide in the general atmosphere *q.v.* comes from the combustion of the sulphur present in most fuels. All the sulphur in oil, and from 80 to 90 per cent of that in coal and coke, is emitted from the chimney as sulphur dioxide, the remainder being retained in the ash.

Sulphur Trioxide A constituent of flue gases from sulphur bearing fuels, frequently to the extent of 3 to 5 per cent of the sulphur dioxide *q.v.* present. Several mechanisms appear to contribute to its formation; in every case a supply of oxygen is necessary. Thus the reduction of excess air tends to inhibit the formation of this corrosion-promoting gas.

Superadiabatic Lapse Rate A lapse rate greater than the dry adiabatic lapse rate, i.e. greater than $10°C$ per kilometre. The dry adiabatic lapse rate is often exceeded by a factor of several times close to a land surface which is strongly heated by solar radiation. Turbulence in the atmosphere is strong and the dilution of waste industrial gases more rapid than in average or neutral conditions.

See Lapse Rates

Surface-water Water which fails to penetrate into the sub-soil and flows along the surface of the ground, eventually entering a lake, river, or creek. It describes water from a perennial flowing stream; water stored behind a rock bar, weir or dam placed across a stream; and water collected from a small drainage area, e.g. a roof, and stored in a tank for domestic use.

See Ground-Water.

Survivorship The proportion of individuals in a community *q.v.* or population *q.v.* surviving to a particular age.

Suspended Solids Solids in a liquid that can be removed through sedimentation or filtration.

Sustained Yield Conservation That aspect of conservation *q.v.* which seeks wise use and continuing productivity of renewable natural resources; originating with forestry, the principle has been extended to other fields.

Swidden Agriculture Also known as "slash and burn', or shifting cultivation or shifting agriculture; a type of agriculture involving the clearing of land by cutting and burning the vegetation to open the soil for planting, it is the major agricultural technique used by the people of Central and South America, Asia, Africa and others parts of the world. After limited use the land is abandoned, and a fresh clearing made elsewhere; thus only a fraction of land area is under cultivation at any one time. Most agriculturists consider swidden agriculture to be wasteful and inefficient, while large amounts of land are required to operate it.

Symbiosis An association of dissimilar organisms whether to their mutual advantage, or otherwise.

Sympatric Populations Populations dispersed over a common area, as distinct from allopatric populations which have different areas of distribution.

Syndrome A set of concurrent symptoms or signs of a disease.

Synecology *See* Biocoenology.

Synergistic Effect The tendency of chemicals and processes to react together to form possibly unforeseen combinations which may have a wholly new or markedly more powerful effect than the substances or processes taken separately. Synergistic effects occur in the formation of photochemical smogs and have been suspected to have occurred also in the London smog episodes of 1952 and 1962. A synergistic effect may link different elements in the total biosphere *q.v.* utilizing, for example, organic substances and the characteristics of light. The formation of highly toxic methyl mercury *q.v.,* through the interaction of organic matter and mercury, is another example of a synergistic effect.

   See Antagonistic Effect, Biological Control.

Systematics A study of the diversity of living organisms; often used synonymously with taxonomy.

T

Tailings Those portions of washed ore that are regarded as too poor to be treated further; also called debris.

   See Mining Wastes.

Tax Incentives for Environment Protection Incentives pro-

vided by governments through tax credits, tax relief, or accelerated depreciation, for the purpose of stimulating investment in pollution control equipment in industrial plants. The Australian Federal Government has strongly resisted special concessions to industry for this purpose, adhering to the principle that the polluter should pay.
See Polluter Pays Principle.

Taxonomy The study of the methods of classifying organisms.

Technological Effects or "real" effects. Effects which alter the total production possibilities or the total welfare opportunities for consumers in the economy. The effects are described as economies when they are favourable, and diseconomies when they are unfavourable. Classical examples of external real diseconomies are air and water pollution; the effects are borne by persons and firms other than those who cause the pollution and in consequence production and consumption opportunities elsewhere in the economy are reduced.

Teleoclimate The micro-climate at the boundary between living organisms and the environment *q.v.*

Temperature Inversion *See* Inversion.

Terpenes A group of volatile aromatic organic substances commonly released from the shoots of flowering plants in particular families.

Terracing An embankment of earth, constructed across a slope in such a way as to control water run-off and minimize erosion. To be effective, terraces must check water flow before it attains sufficient velocity to loosen and transport soil.
See Soil Erosion Control.

Territoriality The identification of an individual organism, population *q.v.* or community *q.v.* with a particular spatial area or volume.

Tertiary Treatment Any sewage purification process which is capable of removing over 98% of the pollutants from sewage, following a secondary treatment plant.

During the past few years several methods by which effluents from percolating filters may be improved or "polished" have been examined. These methods have included the use of microstrainers for the treatment of effluent direct from the filters and the treatment of humus tank effluents by irrigation over land and by passage through slow sand filters, lagoons, or pebble-bed clarifers. Polishing is also described as advanced water treatment or tertiary treatment.

Using a polishing process, a Royal Commission *q.v.* effluent may be much improved, both the BOD and the suspended solids being less than 10 ppm.

Sewage effluent of Royal Commission standard can be made more attractive for many industrial purposes by relatively simple clarification and sterilization processes. For example, treatment by addition of alumina-ferric, followed by sand filtration and chlorination *q.v.* will yield a clear colourless water free from bacterial contamination suitable for many industrial purposes. A fine example of tertiary treatment has been applied to a sewage treatment plant discharging into Lake Tahoe, California. The effluent from the activated sludge plant was endangering the exceptional clarity of the Lake and the addition of nutrients to the Lake was likely to accelerate eutrophication *q.v.* It became necessary to ensure than any effluent discharged was of a standard approaching that of a potable water. A tertiary or polishing treatment was introduced, the activated sludge plant effluent being coagulated with alum in a micro-floc unit with filtration through a mixed media bed. The filtrate then passed through an activated carbon column to give a final effluent of high quality, with a BOD of less than 1 ppm, phosphate and organic nitrogen being reduced to less than 2 ppm.

Rapid sand filters are also used in tertiary treatment. Most of the straining is effected by the top layers of sand. Rapid filters are easier to clean than slow sand filters and the area required is much less. About a 40—70 per cent reduction in BOD and a 70—90 per cent reduction of suspended solids is achieved. Large scale plant is operating at Coventry, Luton and Rye Meads, England. A considerable amount of interest has recently been shown in the application of upflow filtration techniques for the tertiary treatment of sewage works effluent.

See also Humus, Nutrient Stripping, Royal Commission Standards.

Tetra Ethyl Lead   A petroleum additive; since 1923, tetra ethyl lead has been added to petrol to reduce the tendency to 'knocking' or detonation. Since 1959, another anti-knock additive, tetra methyl lead has been added to certain grades of petrol. The amount of additive used has tended to increase. The combustion of leaded petrol is the major source of lead in the atmosphere of urban areas. While the question of the likely hazard to health arising from the inhalation of lead compounds by the public at large remains unresolved, unleaded or low lead gasolines are being introduced in the United States; this decision was based upon the need to remove lead because it reduces the effectiveness of catalytic devices used on cars to restrict the emission of carbon monoxide and hydrocarbons. The use of unleaded or low lead petrol is not without some disadvantages; essentially it implies a reduction of compression ratios to cope with lower octane fuel, accompanied by increased petrol consumption. Conversely, to bring an unleaded fuel up to 90 octane rating (a standard petrol today has an octane rating of about this figure) would involve refiners in additional costs which would be reflected in the price of petrol. It has been considered prudent in Australia to recognize the undesirability of high tetra ethyl lead content in petrol. The Australian Environment Council has adopted a programme for reducing the maximum and average lead content in petrol on a national basis:

	Max. in any sample g/litre	Three-monthly average g/litre
As from 1 January 1973	0.55	0.50
As from 1 January 1977	0.45	0.40

Thermal Pollution   The transfer of heat from industrial processes to bodies of water or air in such quantities as to be detrimental to the environment. Effluents having a significant effect on the temperature of a river may affect the oxygen content of the water and accentuate other adverse conditions. At sufficiently high temperatures, fish may die; fish populations could be destroyed also by the lethal effects of increased temperature either on another

animal on which they feed or on their own spawn. Heat
will accelerate the decomposition processes taking place in
water; in relation to oxygen-sag curves *q.v.*, the effect will
be to lower the curve and also to depress the saturation
line. In the presence of sufficient oxygen, it appears that
heat alone will shorten the stretch of river affected by the
pollution load, accelerating purification. In a river with a
'light' pollution load this would be beneficial; however, in
a river with a 'heavy' pollution load the effect is likely to
be harmful. The harmful effects may include a reduction
of the oxygen concentration in g/m^3 below the level
critical to the organisms living in the water. A sufficient
loss of oxygen will result in anaerobic conditions. Sewage
fungus *q.v.*, found frequently in polluted rivers, grows
rapidly in warmed water.

Power stations use large quantities of water in
condensers for the cooling and condensing of exhaust
steam from the turbines. Two general methods are in use:

Figure 13   High Marnham Power Station, near Newark, Nottinghamshire, England. A 1,000 MW coal-fired power station, equipped with
five natural-draught cooling towers each 105 metres in height. The two
chimneys are 138 metres in height. Officially opened in 1962, High
Marnham was the first 1,000 MW power station to be commissioned in
Britain. The cooling-tower make-up water is obtained from the River
Trent. (Source: Central Electricity Generating Board, London)

1. Direct cooling, in which water is pumped from a river or other source, used once for cooling purposes, and returned at once to the sea, river, estuary or lake. In passing through the condensers, the temperature of the water is usually raised by about 10° C.

2. Indirect cooling, in which water is pumped from a river or other source, used many times for cooling purposes, and is finally dissipated to the general atmosphere as steam from large open cooling towers. The use of large cooling towers, common in Britain, to dissipate the recovered waste heat eliminates the thermal pollution problem. However, make-up water for a cooling tower system is taken from the river or stream, eliminating its subsequent use by those down-river.

See Figure 13.

Thermocline or metalimnion. The middle stratum of water in a lake, below the epilimnion *q.v.* and above the hypolimnion *q.v.*, typified by a temperature gradient of more than one degree C per metre of depth.

Therophyte An annual plant, i.e. a plant that completes its life cycle within one season, surviving the subsequent unfavourable period as a dormant seed.

Threshold of Hearing The pressure at which a sound source, in the absence of background noise, first becomes audible. In the average young adult with normal hearing, it has been found to be a sound pressure of approximately 0.00002 N/m^2 in the frequency region of greatest sensitivity (around 3,000 Hz). As the sound pressure increases, the sound becomes louder until at a pressure of approximately 20 N/m^2 the sound can be almost "felt". This is known as the "threshold of feeling". Thus the amplitude of sound pressures in the audible range, from the threshold of hearing to the threshold of feeling, varies enormously. To present this variation in a more convenient scale, a logarithmic unit was first chosen, known as the bel; subsequently, the decibel (dB), which is one-tenth of a bel, came into common use.

See Decibel A (dBA) Scale, Sound Wave.

Tokyo—Yokohama Respiratory Disease (T—YRD) Originally called Tokyo—Yokohama Asthma, a respiratory complaint associated with the Kanto Plain or Tokyo—

Yokohama area. Surrounded by a mountain barrier to the north and west, and the ocean to the east and south, the Kanto Plain suffers a severe air pollution *q.v.* problem; most industry is located near the sea and burns fuel oil and soft coal. The complaint is characterized by severe cough, wheezing, persistent shortness of breath and reduced oxygen uptake. However, most sufferers are cigarette smokers, indicating a combined overburdening of the system. The only satisfactory method of treatment has been the removal of the patient from the area.

Torrey Canyon Disaster   An incident which occurred on 18 March 1967, when the Liberian oil tanker *Torrey Canyon* went aground on the Seven Stones reef, about 24 kilometres northeast of the Scilly Isles, liberating her cargo of Kuwait crude oil. On the afternoon of 24 March, there was a slick of oil some 64 kilometres long off Lands End with an average width of perhaps 16 kilometres. Initially, detergent was sprayed on the oil floating on the sea to emulsify and "sink" it. Subsequently, the ship was bombed, some of the oil being burned, the remainder being swept away by the sea. The burning consumed perhaps one-third of the total cargo. A great deal of the oil finally landed on the Cornish beaches; this too was very largely dealt with by the use of a solvent emulsifier mixture. Some of the oil drifted across the English Channel necessitating prompt action by the French Government to safeguard the beaches and oyster fisheries of Britanny. This major disaster alerted all countries to the dangers.

See Oil Pollution.

Total Pollution Loading   A concept which regards the aggregate mass of a specific pollutant, discharged to the environment *q.v.* in a given time period, as more important than the concentration of a pollutant as a basis of environment protection legislation. The total loading on any one segment of the environment becomes the basis of control. In contrast, the measurements proposed in the Eighth Report of the British Royal Commission of 1913 relating to sewage effluents, and widely adopted in Australia, are concerned with the concentrations only of certain pollutants in effluents.

See Royal Commission Standards.

Town and Country Planning Community planning of developments in town and country with the aim of achieving a socially desirable balance between the many competing uses to which land may be put, and to ensure that public and private development is carried out with the least possible harm to amenities. Planning activities in the United Kingdom have included:

1. the provision of urban amenities in the country-side for the agricultural population
2. the preservation of historical monuments and the creation of national parks
3. schemes for the redistribution of industry and the building of new towns
4. the creation of green belts to restrain the outside spread of towns and cities
5. slum clearance and development schemes
6. the provision of sports facilities, airfields and highways.
   See also Land-Use.

Toxic Capable, through chemical action, of killing, injuring, or impairing an organism.

Trade Wastes Wastes of organic and inorganic origin discharged by industrial and commerical enterprises. Organic wastes are discharged on a considerable scale by the food industries: canneries, dairies, breweries, abattoirs, and fish-meat factories. Other contributors include paper-mills, tanneries, petro-chemical works, textile manufacturers, and laundries. Inorganic wastes include acids, alkalis, cyanides, sulphides, and the salts of arsenic, lead, copper, chromium, and zinc.
See also Water Pollution.

Transfer Facility A facility operated for the purpose of transferring refuse from collection trucks and other vehicles to larger-capacity trucks. The larger trucks transport the refuse to a disposal site. The purpose of this arrangement is to assist in minimizing overall collection and disposal costs per ton of refuse handled.
See also Solid Waste Management.

Trickling Filter Or biological filter, an aerobic process used in secondary treatment *q.v.* plants for the processing of sewage. Trickling filters consist of beds of coarse material (generally 50 to 100 mm crushed stone) over which the sewage is sprinkled at a uniform rate; they are generally not less than two metres deep and circular in plan. Settled sewage may be applied to the bed either by mechanical distributors or by fixed nozzles so designed and spaced as to ensure proper distribution of the sewage over the whole area of the bed. The use of plastic (polyvinyl chloride) shapes instead of stones in the beds of trickling filters roughly doubles the surface area on which the biological process takes place. The efficiency of standard trickling filters varies from 85 to 95 per cent BOD reduction, 90 to 95 per cent suspended solids removal, and from 80 to 99 per cent bacteria removal. This secondary stage may be followed by tertiary treatment *q.v.*

Trophic Pertaining to nutrition.

Trophic Level A particular step occupied by a population *q.v.* in the process of energy transfer within an ecosystem *q.v.*

Troposphere The lower layer of the atmosphere *q.v.*, extending up to about 11 kilometres above the surface of the earth and in which temperature normally falls with increasing height.

Trunk Sewer A major sewer collecting flows from a large area, e.g. the southeastern outfall main or trunk sewer in Melbourne.

Tunnelling A form of erosion related especially to one kind of soil; the erosion goes on below the surface and may not show until the surface collapses into the tunnel. The subsurface disperses during wet weather, a mud spring appearing at a point lower down the slope. In this way, a whole hillside may become underminded. An initial counter-measure is to keep a cover of vegetation.
    See Soil Erosion.

Turbidity Visible pollution due to suspended material in water causing a reduction in the transmissionof light.

Turbulence The random movements of the air which are superimposed upon the mean wind speed. Individual movement is called a turbulent eddy which may have almost any size and may move in any direction at any speed.
    See Meteorological Influences.

U

Underground Water Water other than surface-water *q.v.* being drawn from relatively shallow wells or boreholes, and from deep artesian bores.

United Nations Conference on the Human Environment, 1972 Held in Stockholm, from 5 to 16 June 1972, the first United Nations Conference on the Human Environment; the main purpose of the Conference was defined as being: 'to serve as a practical means to encourage, and to provide guidelines for, action by Government and international organizations designed to protect and improve the human environment and to remedy and prevent its impairment, by means of international co-operation, bearing in mind the particular importance of enabling developing countries to forestall occurrence of such problems.'. The Conference was attended by 113 delegations. The principal achievements of the Conference were the agreements reached on:

1. A Declaration on the Human Environment (*See* Appendix)
2. An extensive programme of international action (the Action Plan)
3. A permanent environment secretariat (now based in Nairobi, Kenya)
4. An environment fund of $US 100m for expenditure in the first five years to support new environmental initiatives.

The major disappointment of the Conference was the failure of the Soviet Union and countries from eastern Europe, with the exception of Yugoslavia and Rumania, to attend. The Conference was attended, however, by China.

Urban and Regional Planning That part of resource management which is concerned with spatial ordering in the urban and regional environments.

Urban Renewal The renovation of the decaying central areas of cities by the demolition or up-grading of existing dwellings, reduction of street congestion, and general improvement in environmental conditions.

Urbanization A process leading to a societal change, characterized by the movement of people from rural to urban areas. Urban areas have become increasingly densely populated, with towns becoming closely linked to form agglomerates, city regions, urban zones and conurbations. Australia is one of the most urbanized nations in the world. In 1966, 82.9 per cent of the population was classified as urbanized; by 1971, the proportion had risen to 85.6 per cent.

V

Vadose Water   Water that is present between the water-table *q.v.* and the surface of the earth.

   See Ground-Water, Surface-Water.

Value Judgment   A statement of preference; if a person says "I prefer A to B" this is a personal value judgment. If A is considered generally to be better than B, this is a community value judgment, or common value. Value judgments are judgments in the realm of ethics; with such judgments one may agree or disagree, but they can never be classified as correct or incorrect.

Vasomotor   Having an effect on the calibre of blood vessels.

Veering Wind   The clockwise change of direction of a wind, e.g. from N through NE; an opposite change of direction to backing. The same definition applies whether in the northern or southern hemisphere.

Virus   A filterable micro-organism, invisible by ordinary microscopy, capable of multiplying locally in the cells of the body and forming inclusion bodies in the cells; a virus disease is one caused by a virus. There is general agreement that present sewage treatment *q.v.* processes do not entirely remove the virus hazard, although some studies indicate that if chlorination *q.v.* is used efficiently and earlier treatment stages are adequate, the virus hazard is considerably reduced. Most of the human faecal or enteric viruses found in sewage are enterovirus members of the picornavirus group (polio, coxsackie and echo viruses); they fall in the size range 23—30 nanometres.

Visual Environment   Those aspects of the environment with which the eye is either pleased or offended. The visual environment is impaired by overhead services, intrusive hoardings, poor external appearances to new buildings, central city dilapidation, visible discharges to air or water, and disruption of the countryside or beaches by mining operations. In recent years, land subdividers and some local councils have introduced underground electricity supply to an increasing number of new housing estates. Underground distribution is two to three times dearer than overhead systems due to the need for heavy insulation. With underground distribution it is less easy to progressively increase the load-carrying capacity of the lines, so that careful long-term planning is needed at the outset. A balance has to be found between providing for load-growth and the dis-economy of having substantial unused capacity for a long time. By June, 1973, Melbourne had only 2000 housing lots serviced by underground reticulation. Underground distribution removes not only unsightly "wirescape", but also obtrusive overhead transformers.

Viviparous Descriptive of an animal that produces living offspring instead of eggs, i.e. nearly all mammals; also descriptive of plants which produce bulbils or small plants instead of, or in addition to, seeds.

W

Wallace's Line The division between the Australasian and Oriental biogeographical regions; it extends from south of the Philippines, passing between Borneo and the Celebes, and between Lombok and Bali. It follows a deep trough in the ocean floor between Borneo and New Guinea. Regarded as a transitional zone rather than a sharp division.

Washout The process of scavenging the atmosphere *q.v.* by precipitation.

Waste Any matter, whether liquid, solid, gaseous, or radioactive, which is discharged, emitted, or deposited in the environment in such volume, constituency or manner as to cause an alteration of the environment. The concept of a waste embraces all unwanted and economically unusable by-products at any given place and time, and any other matter which may be discharged, accidentally or otherwise, to the environment.

See Re-Cycling.

Waste Management The current term describing a comprehensive, integrated, and rational systems approach towards the achievement and maintenance of acceptable environmental quality. It involves preparing policies; determining environmental standards; fixing emission rates; enforcing regulations; monitoring air, water, and soil quality, and noise emissions; and offering advice to government, industry, land developers and public.

Waterborne Diseases Diseases such as cholera, typhoid fever, dysentery, gastroenteritis, hepatitis and bilharziasis, which are commonly transmitted through contaminated water supplies. While the classical water-borne diseases have been virtually eradicated from many of the developed countries, these diseases are still endemic in other parts of the world. Bilharziasis (caused by schistosomes or blood flukes) is commonly transmitted in tropical countries by bathing in polluted canal water. Urban filariasis (caused by filariae or nematode worms and associated, inter alia, with elephantiasis) is transmitted by the bile of an insect vector that breeds in polluted water. Although water transmission is thought to cause only a very small fraction of the disease hepatitis, nevertheless a major epidemic of infectious hepatitis did occur in New Delhi, India, in 1955 in circumstances suggesting that the treatment of highly polluted water had been successful in controlling bacteria, but not the hepatitus virus. An epidemic of gastroenteritis occurred in the spring of 1965 in Riverside, California; it was estimated that as many as 10,000 to 15,000 people may have been affected. The cause was finally traced to the water supply which was found to contain the bacterium Salmonella Typhimurium. The community water supply, from deep wells inside and outside the city, had never been chlorinated and was subject to the risk of contamination in the distribution system. The Aberdeen typhoid outbreak of 1964 is thought to have been caused by a tin of corned beef infected by untreated river water used in the factory for cooling tins after sterilization; the water was probably contaminated by an Argentinian typhoid carrier. Shellfish, particularly oysters, are notorious vectors of typhoid; oysters growing in river estuaries contaminated by sewage filter organic particles, including Salmonella typhosa, from the water. While the organism lodges in the oyster. the oyster itself is not affected by it.

See Water Pollution.

Water-formed Deposits Any accumulation of insoluble material derived or deposited from water, or formed by the reaction of water with the surfaces with which it comes into contact; deposits may be classified as corrosion products, biological deposits, scale or sludge.

Water Pollution Substances, bacteria or viruses present in such concentrations or numbers as to impair the quality of the water rendering it less suitable or unsuitable for its intended use and presenting a hazard to man or to his environment. Pollution may be caused by:

1. Bacteria, viruses and other organisms that can cause disease, e.g. cholera, typhoid fever, and dysentery
2. Inorganic salts that cannot be removed by any simple conventional treatment process, making the water less suitable for drinking, for irrigation and for many industries
3. Plant nutrients such as potash, phosphates, and nitrates which, while largely inorganic salt, have the added effect of increasing weed growth, promoting algal blooms and producing, by photosynthesis, organic matter which may settle to the bottom of a lake
4. Oily materials that may be inimical to fish life, cause unsightliness, screen the river surface from the air thus reducing re-oxygenation, accumulate in troublesome quantities, or have a high oxygen demand
5. Specific toxic agents, ranging from metal salts to complex synthetic chemicals
6. Waste heat that may render the river less suitable for certain purposes
7. Silt that may enter a river in large quantities causing changes in the character of the river bed
8. Radioactive substances.

See also Algae, Bilharziasis, Coliform Bacteria, Eutrophication, Oil Pollution, Pollution, Radioactivity, River Thames Clean-Up, Sewage Treatment, Thermal Pollution, Virus, Water-Borne Diseases. *Also* Table 3.

Elements or substances	Indicator substances
Arsenic (As, particularly As_2O_3)	Alkylbenzene sulphonates, ABS (index of pollution by all synthetic detergents)
Barium (Ba)	
Cadmium (Cd)	Carbon chloroform extract, CCE (Includes most organic compounds, including organic carcinogens and pesticides)
Chlorine (Cl_2) (with reaction products from organic pollutants may have toxic potential)	
Chromium (CrO_3)	Phenol (includes phenols, cresols and homologues)
Fluoride (F)	Total dissolved solids, TDS (includes minerals contributing to "hardness")
Lead (Pb)	
Mercury (Hg)	Gross β-radiation (index of mixed radioisotopes in the absence of ^{90}Sr and α-enitters)
Nitrate (NO_3)	
Selenium (SeO_2, SeO_3)	
Vanadium (V)	

Table 3 Selected water pollutants having potential long term effects (Source: World Health Organisation, *Research Into Environmental Pollution*, Technical Report Series No. 406, Geneva: 1968

Watershed The elevated boundary line separating the head-streams which are tributary to different river systems or catchment *q.v.* basins; also called a water-parting or divide.

Water-Table The surface of the ground-water *q.v.*; the upper surface of a zone of saturation, save where that surface is formed by an impermeable layer or stratum. The surface is uneven and variable; during wet weather it tends to rise, falling during dry weather. The lowest level to which a water-table falls in any locality is known as the permanent water-table.

Wealth In economic science, goods and other assets in existence at any time which command a market value (i.e. a price) if offered for sale; this implies that such assets have utility and scarcity value, and that it is possible to transfer their ownership from one person or body to another. Economic science has been largely concerned with the production and distribution of wealth defined in this way, and not with assets which have value in the mind of the owner only. Wealth is a fund of goods that can be consumed; it represents stored-up facilities for the satisfaction of future wants. Economists also recognise "free goods" which do not normally command a price, such as air and water, but which may still be essential to human welfare. In more recent years, economists have given greater attention to social costs and social benefits which embrace many matters not falling within the conventional measuring rod of money.

Weather The condition of the atmosphere *q.v.* at a certain time or over a certain short period as described by various meteorological phenomena such as atmospheric pressure, temperature, humidity, rainfall, cloudiness, and wind speed and direction.

See also Climate.

Wildlife A collective term embracing several thousand different species of mammals, birds and reptiles. No two species respond in precisely the same manner and degree to the influences of the environment *q.v.*; the differences in response are aspects of competition, selection and evolution.

Wind Rose A diagram indicating the frequency and strengths of winds in a definite locality for a given period of years. It is conventional to consider the wind direction as the direction from which the wind blows, e.g. a northeast wind will carry pollutants to the southwest of the source.

See Prevailing Wind.

Winds Ordered horizontal air motions; known as advection. Vertical motions are called convection, while turbulence describes the chaotic motion of air in all directions.

World Environment Day The fifth of June each year was adopted by the United Nations Conference on the Human Environment, 1972 *q.v.* to mark the beginning of the First Conference and as a means of focussing attention on national and world environment problems.

X

Xeromorphic Applied to plants which appear to have the ability to restrict water loss during adverse conditions; a plant displaying this characteristic is described as a xerophyte.

Xerophyte A plant which is adapted to living in a region where drought conditions normally prevail; its structure is modified to obtain and conserve a maximum amount of water.

Xerothermic Period A historical period of warm-dry climate; there is evidence of at least one such period during the holocene period.

    See Geological Time Scale.

X-Ray Electromagnetic radiation of short wavelength.

    See Radioactivity.

Y

Yokkaichi Asthma Severe asthma caused by oxides of sulphur in Yokkaichi, site of the largest petrochemical complex in Japan.

Z

Zimmerman Process A sewage treatment process achieving oxidation of organic material in a closed vessel under high pressure and temperature.

Zoophyte An animal which resembles a plant, e.g. a sponge or a Coral Polyp.

Zooplankton or protozoa *q.v.* Minute unicellular animals (crustacae, etc.) often in the stage of larvae, which swim or float suspended in water.

Appendix

The United Nations Conference on the Human Environment

Having met at Stockholm from 5 to 16 June 1972,

Having considered the need for a common outlook and for common principles to inspire and guide the peoples of the world in the preservation and enhancement of the human environment,

I

Proclaims that:

1. Man is both creature and moulder of his environment, which gives him physical sustenance and affords him the opportunity for intellectual, moral, social and spiritual growth. In the long and tortuous evolution of the human race on this planet a stage has been reached when, through the rapid acceleration of science and technology, man has acquired the power to transform his environment in countless ways on an unprecedented scale. Both aspects of man's environment, the natural and the man-made, are essential to his well-being and to the enjoyment of basic human rights — even the right to life itself.

2. The protection and improvement of the human environment is a major issue which affects the well-being of peoples and economic development throughout the world; it is the urgent desire of the people of the whole world and the duty of all Governments.

3. Man has constantly to sum up experience and go on discovering, inventing, creating and advancing. In our time, man's capability to transform his surroundings, if used wisely, can bring to all peoples the benefits of development and the opportunity to enhance the quality of life. Wrongly or heedlessly applied, the same power can do incalculable harm to human beings and the human environment. We see around us growing evidence of man-made harm in many regions of the earth: dangerous levels of pollution in water,

air, earth and living beings; major and undesirable distur-
bances to the ecological balance of the biosphere; destruction
and depletion of irreplaceable resources; and gross deficiencies harmful to the physical, mental and social health of man,
in the man-made environment, particularly in the living and
working environment.

4. In the developing countries most of the environmental
problems are caused by under-development. Millions
continue to live far below the minimum levels required for a
decent human existence, deprived of adequate food and
clothing, shelter and education, health and sanitation. Therefore, the developing countries must direct their efforts to
development, bearing in mind their priorities and the need to
safeguard and improve the environment. For the same
purpose, the industrialized countries should make efforts to
reduce the gap between themselves and the developing
countries. In the industrialized countries, environmental
problems are generally related to industrialization and
technological development.

5. The natural growth of population continuously
presents problems on the preservation of the environment,
and adequate policies and measures should be adopted, as
appropriate, to face these problems. Of all things in the
world, people are the most precious. It is the people that
propel social progress, create social wealth, develop science
and technology and, through their hard work, continuously
transform the human environment. Along with social
progress and the advance of production, science and technology, the capability of man to improve the environment
increases with each passing day.

6. A point has been reached in history when we must
shape our actions throughout the world with a more prudent
care for their environmental consequences. Through
ignorance or indifference we can do massive and irreversible
harm to the earthly environment on which our life and well-
being depend. Conversely, through fuller knowledge and
wiser action, we can achieve for ourselves and our posterity a
better life in an environment more in keeping with human
needs and hopes. There are broad vistas for the enhancement
of environmental quality and the creation of a good life.

What is needed is an enthusiastic but calm state of mind and intense but orderly work. For the purpose of attaining freedom in the world of nature, man must use knowledge to build, in collaboration with nature, a better environment. To defend and improve the human environment for present and future generations has become an imperative goal for mankind — a goal to be pursued together with, and in harmony with, the established and fundamental goals of peace and of world-wide economic and social development.

7. To achieve this environmental goal will demand the acceptance of responsibility by citizens and communities and by enterprises and institutions at every level, all sharing equitably in common efforts. Individuals in all walks of life as well as organizations in many fields, by their values and the sum of their actions, will shape the world environment of the future. Local and national governments will bear the greatest burden for large-scale environmental policy and action within their jurisdictions. International co-operation is also needed in order to raise resources to support the developing countries in carrying out their responsibilities in this field. A growing class of environmental problems, because they are regional or global in extent or because they affect the common international realm, will require extensive co-operation among nations and action by international organizations in the common interest. The Conference calls upon Governments and peoples to exert common efforts for the preservation and improvement of the human environment, for the benefit of all the people and for their posterity.

II

PRINCIPLES

States the common conviction that:

PRINCIPLE 1

Man has the fundamental right to freedom, equality and adequate conditions of life, in an environment of a quality that permits a life of dignity and well-being, and he bears a solemn responsibility to protect and improve the environment for present and future generations. In this respect, policies promoting or perpetuating *apartheid*, racial segregation, discrimination, colonial and other forms of oppression and foreign domination stand condemned and must be eliminated.

PRINCIPLE 2

The natural resources of the earth including the air, water, land, flora and fauna and especially representative samples of natural ecosystems must be safeguarded for the benefit of present and future generations through careful planning or management, as appropriate.

PRINCIPLE 3

The capacity of the earth to produce vital renewable resources must be maintained and, wherever practicable, restored or improved.

PRINCIPLE 4

Man has a special responsibility to safeguard and wisely manage the heritage of wildlife and its habitats which are now gravely imperilled by a combination of adverse factors. Nature conservation including wildlife must therefore receive importance in planning for economic development.

PRINCIPLE 5

The non-renewable resources of the earth must be employed in such a way as to guard against the danger of their future exhaustion and to ensure that benefits from such employment are shared by all mankind.

PRINCIPLE 6

The discharge of toxic substances or of other substances and the release of heat, in such quantities or concentrations as to exceed the capacity of the environment to render them harmless, must be halted in order to ensure that serious or irreversible damage is not inflicted upon ecosystems. The just struggle of the peoples of all countries against pollution should be supported.

PRINCIPLE 7

States shall take all possible steps to prevent pollution of the seas by substances that are liable to create hazards to human health, to harm living resources and marine life, to damage amenities or to interfere with other legitimate uses of the sea.

PRINCIPLE 8

Economic and social development is essential for ensuring a favourable living and working environment for man and for creating conditions on earth that are necessary for the improvement of the quality of life.

PRINCIPLE 9

Environmental deficiencies generated by the conditions of underdevelopment and natural disasters pose grave problems and can best be remedied by accelerated development through the transfer of substantial quantities of financial and technological assistance as a supplement to the domestic effort of the developing countries and such timely assistance as may be required.

PRINCIPLE 10

For the developing countries, stability of prices and adequate earnings for primary commodities and raw material are essential to environmental management since economic factors as well as ecological processes must be taken into account.

PRINCIPLE 11

The environmental policies of all States should enhance and not adversely affect the present or future development potential of developing countries, nor should they hamper the attainment of better living conditions for all, and appropriate steps should be taken by States and international organizations with a view to reaching agreement on meeting the possible national and international economic consequences resulting from the application of environmental measures.

PRINCIPLE 12

Resources should be made available to preserve and

improve the environment, taking into account the circumstances and particular requirements of developing countries and any costs which may emanate from their incorporating environmental safeguards into their development planning and the need for making available to them, upon their request, additional international technical and financial assistance for this purpose.

PRINCIPLE 13

In order to achieve a more rational management of resources and thus to improve the environment, States should adopt an integrated and co-ordinated approach to their development planning so as to ensure that development is compatible with the need to protect and improve the human environment for the benefit of their population.

PRINCIPLE 14

Rational planning constitutes an essential tool for reconciling any conflict between the needs of development and the need to protect and improve the environment.

PRINCIPLE 15

Planning must be applied to human settlements and urbanization with a view to avoiding adverse effects on the environment and obtaining maximum social, economic and environmental benefits for all. In this respect projects which are designed for colonialist and racist domination must be abandoned.

PRINCIPLE 16

Demographic policies, which are without prejudice to basic human rights and which are deemed appropriate by Governments concerned, should be applied in those regions where the rate of population growth or excessive population concentrations are likely to have adverse effects on the environment or development, or where low population density may prevent improvement of the human environment and impede development.

PRINCIPLE 17

Appropriate national institutions must be entrusted with the task of planning, managing or controlling the environmental resources of States with the view to enhancing environmental quality.

PRINCIPLE 18

Science and technology, as part of their contribution to economic and social development, must be applied to the identification, avoidance and control of environmental risks and the solution of environmental problems and for the common good of mankind.

PRINCIPLE 19

Education in environmental matters, for the younger generation as well as adults, giving due consideration to the underprivileged, is essential in order to broaden the basis for an enlightened opinion and responsible conduct by individuals, enterprises and communities in protecting and improving the environment in its full human dimension. It is also essential that mass media of communications avoid contributing to the deterioration of the environment, but, on the contrary, disseminate information of an educational nature, on the need to protect and improve the environment in order to enable man to develop in every respect.

PRINCIPLE 20

Scientific research and development in the context of environmental problems, both national and multinational, must be promoted in all countries, especially the developing countries. In this connexion, the free flow of up-to-date scientific information and transfer of experience must be supported and assisted, to facilitate the solution of environmental problems; environmental technologies should be made available to developing countries on terms which would encourage their wide dissemination without constituting an economic burden on the developing countries.

PRINCIPLE 21

States have, in accordance with the Charter of the United

Nations and the principles of international law, the sovereign right to exploit their own resources pursuant to their own environmental policies, and the responsibility to ensure that activities within their jurisdiction or control do not cause damage to the environment of other States or of areas beyond the limits of national jurisdiction.

PRINCIPLE 22

States shall co-operate to develop further the international law regarding liability and compensation for the victims of pollution and other environmental damage caused by activities within the jurisdiction or control of such States to areas beyond their jurisdiction.

PRINCIPLE 23

Without prejudice to such criteria as may be agreed upon by the international community, or to standards which will have to be determined nationally, it will be essential in all cases to consider the systems of values prevailing in each country, and the extent of the applicability of standards which are valid for the most advanced countries but which may be inappropriate and of unwarranted social cost for the developing countries.

PRINCIPLE 24

International matters concerning the protection and improvement of the environment should be handled in a co-operative spirit by all countries, big or small, on an equal footing. Co-operation through multilateral or bilateral arrangements or other appropriate means is essential to effectively control, prevent, reduce and eliminate adverse environmental effects resulting from activities conducted in all spheres, in such a way that due account is taken of the sovereignty and interests of all States.

PRINCIPLE 25

States shall ensure that international organizations play a co-ordinated, efficient and dynamic role for the protection and improvement of the environment.

PRINCIPLE 26

Man and his environment must be spared the effects of nuclear weapons and all other means of mass destruction. States must strive to reach prompt agreement, in the relevant international organs, on the elimination and complete destruction of such weapons.

Bibliography

GENERAL

American Chemical Society. *Cleaning Our Environment : The Chemical Bases for Action* Washington, D.C. : American Chemical Society, 1969.

Australian House of Representatives. *Report of the Committee on the Problem of the Crown-of-Thorns Starfish.* Canberra: 1971.

Australian Conservation Foundation Publications:

Occasional Series

No. 2 Conservation as an Emerging Concept, by Judith Wright.
No. 4 The Commercial Hunting of Kangaroos, by Dr. Francis Ratcliffe.
No. 5 Preservation of Diversity, by Sir Garfield Barwick.
No. 7 Economic Growth and the Environment, by Sir Garfield Barwick.
No. 8 Management of Conservation Reserves, by Drs. R. G. Downes, H. J. Frith, D. F. McMichael.
No. 9 Matching Ecological & Economic Realities, by Dr. H. C. Coombs.

Viewpoint Series

No. 1 Conservation of Kangaroos
No. 2 Waterfowl Conservation
No. 5 Bushfire Control and Conservation
No. 6 Conservation and Mining in Modern Australia
No. 7 Mangroves and Man

Special Publications Series

No. 6 Environmental Pollution — papers of a symposium
No. 7 Conservation of the Australian Coast — papers of a symposium
No. 8 Conservation and Mining — papers of a symposium.

Other Publications

Pedder Papers. *Anatomy of a Decision.*
The Future of Lake Pedder — Report of the Lake Pedder Committee of Enquiry, June 1973.

Baldwin, W. and Page, J. K. eds. *Law and the Environment.* New York: Walker, 1970.

Barr, J. *Derelict Britain.* London: Penguin Books, 1969.

Boughey, A. S. *Fundamental Ecology,* Intext Series in Ecology. Scranton: Intext Educational Publishers, 1971.

Carson, R. *Silent Spring.* Boston: Houghton Mifflin, 1962.

Clark, L. R., Geier, P. W., Hughes, R. D., Morris, R. F., *The Ecology of Insect Populations in Theory and Practice.* London: Methuen, 1967.

Bibliography

Commoner, B. *The Closing Circle.* New York: Alfred A. Knopf, 1972.

Costin, A. B. and Frith, H. J. eds. *Conservation.* Australia: Penguin Books , 1971.

Council on Environmental Quality. *Environmental Quality,* Annual Reports. Washington D.C.: U.S. Government Printing Office, 1970 onwards.

Darling, F. F. *Wilderness and Plenty.* Boston: Houghton Mifflin, 1970.

Dempsey, R. ed. *The Politics of Finding Out: Environmental Problems in Australia.* Melbourne: Cheshire, 1974.

Department of Education and Science. *Further Review of Certain Persistent Organochlorine Pesticides Used in Great Britain,* Advisory Committee on Pesticides and Other Toxic Chemicals. London: H.M.S.O., 1970.

Department of the Interior. *Effects of Pesticides on Fish and Wild Life.* Washington, D.C.: U.S. Government Printing Office, 1964.

Detwyler, T. R. ed. *Man's Impact on Environment.* New York: McGraw-Hill, 1971.

Ehrlich P. R. and A. H. *Population, Resources, Environment.* San Francisco: W. H. Freeman, 1970.

Flawn, P. T. *Environmental Geology: Conservation, Land-Use Planning, and Resource Management.* New York: Harper and Row, 1970.

Frith, H. J. *Wildlife Conservation.* Sydney: Angus and Robertson, 1973.

International Atomic Energy Agency. *Environmental Contamination by Radioactive Materials,* Seminar Proceedings, Vienna: 1969.

International Bank for Reconstruction and Development. *Report on the Limits of Growth: A Study by a Special Task Force of the World Bank.* Washington, D.C.: 1972.

Leeper, G. W. ed. *The Australian Environment.* 4th ed., Melbourne: Commonwealth Scientific and Industrial Research Organisation and Melbourne University Press, 1970.

Kneese, A. V., Rolfe, S. E., and Harned, J. W. eds. *Managing the Environment.* New York: Praeger Publishers, 1971.

Meadows, D. H. and others. *The Limits of Growth: A Report for the Club of Rome's Project on the Predicament of Mankind.* London: Earth Island, 1972.

Mellanby, K. *Pesticides and Pollution.* London: Collins, 1969.

Ministry of Defence. *Report of a Working Party on the Transport of Nerve Agents from Nancekuke to Porton and the Disposal of Effluent from Nerve Agent Production.* London: H.M.S.O., 1970.

Owen, O. S. *Natural Resource Conservation: An Ecological Approach.* New York: Macmillan, 1971.

The Public Interest Research Group. *Legalised Pollution: Report on Pollution Control Laws in Queensland.* Brisbane: University of Queensland Press, 1973.

Report of the Committee of Enquiry Appointed by The Honourable The Premier of Victoria to enquire into the Effects of Pesticides. Melbourne: Government Printer, 1966.

Report of the Committee of Inquiry into the National Estate. Canberra: Commonwealth Government Printer, 1974.

Royal Commission on Environmental Pollution.
First Report, Cmnd. 4585, 1971
Second Report, Cmnd. 4894, 1972
Third Report, Cmnd. 5054, 1972
London: H.M.S.O.

Royal Ministry for Foreign Affairs. *Management of Land and Water Resources.* Stockholm: 1972.

Royal Ministry for Foreign Affairs. *Urbanisation and Planning in Sweden.* Stockholm: 1972.

Royal Society of Health. *Radiation Levels in Air, Water and Food.* London: 1964.

Smith, R. L. ed. *The Ecology of Man: An Ecosystem Approach.* New York: Harper and Row, 1972.

Summary Report of Australian Delegation to the United Nations Conference on the Human Environment, Stockholm 5 to 16 June, 1972. Canberra: Commonwealth Government Printer, 1972.

Ward, B. and Dubos, R. *Only One Earth: The Care and Maintenance of a Small Planet.* London: Penguin Books, 1972.

The White House. *Restoring the Quality of Our Environment.* Washington D.C.: U.S. Government Printing Office, 1965.

White Paper. *The Protection of the Environment: The Fight Against Pollution,* Cmnd. 4373. London: H.M.S.O., 1970.

ECONOMICS

Barnett, H. J. and Morse, C. *Scarcity and Growth: The Economics of Natural Resource Availability.* Washington, D.C.: Resources for the Future. 1963.

Bradley, R. M. and Isaac, P. C. G. *Capital and Operating Costs of Sewage Treatment.* Newcastle-Upon-Tyne: Oriel Press, 1969.

Clawson, M., Held, R. B., and Stoddard, C. H. *Land for the Future.* Baltimore: Johns Hopkins Press, 1962.

Dorfman, R. ed. *Measuring Benefits of Government Investment.* Washington, D.C.: Brookings Institution, 1965.

Environmental Protection Agency. *The Economics of Clean Air.* Washington, D.C.: U.S. Government Printing Office, 1972.

Herfindahl, O. C. and Kneese, A. V. *Quality of the Environment: An Economic Approach to Some Problems in Using Land, Water and Air.* Baltimore: Johns Hopkins Press, 1965.

Higbee, E. *A Question of Priorities: New Strategies for Our Urbanised World.* New York: W. Morrow, 1970.

Hirschleifer, J., Milliman, J. W. and De Haven, J. C. *Water Supply: Economics, Technology and Policy.* Chicago: University of Chicago, 1960.

Kneese, A. V., Ayres, R. V., and D'Arge, R. C. *Economics and the Environment: A Materials Balance Approach.* Washington, D.C.: Resources for the Future, 1970.

Kneese, A. V. *Water Pollution: Economic Aspects in Research Needs.* Washington, D.C.: Resources for the Future, 1962.

Krutilla, J. V. and Eclestern, O. *Multiple Purpose River Development: Studies in Applied Economic Analysis.* Baltimore: Johns Hopkins Press, 1958.

Jarrett, H. ed. *Perspectives on Conservation: Essays on America's natural resources based on the Resources for The Future Forum Lectures of 1958.* Baltimore: Johns Hopkins Press, 1958, reprinted 1962.

Marglin, S. A. *Public Investment Criteria: Benefit-Cost Analysis for Planned Economic Growth.* London: Allen and Unwin, 1966.

Mishan, E. J. *The Costs of Economic Growth.* London: Penguin Books, 1967.

Pigou, A. C. *The Economics of Welfare.* 3rd ed., London: Macmillan, 1950.

Treasury Economic Paper No. 2. *Economic Growth: Is It Worth Having?* Canberra: Commonwealth Government Printer, 1973.

Wolozin, H. ed. *The Economics of Air Pollution: A Symposium.* New York: W. A. Norton, 1966.

AIR POLLUTION CONTROL

Annual Reports. The Air Pollution Council of Queensland. Brisbane: Government Printer, 1971 onwards.

Clean Air Society of Australia and New Zealand. *Proceedings of International Clean Air Conference, Melbourne, 15–18 May, 1972.* Melbourne: Clean Air Society, 1972.

Committee on Public Works, U.S. Senate. *Air Quality Criteria.* Washington, D.C.: U.S. Government Printing Office, 1968.

Department of the Environment, *Annual Reports on Alkali, Etc., Works by the Chief Inspectors.* London: H.M.S.O.

Gilpin, A. *Air Pollution.* Brisbane: University of Queensland Press, 1971.

Gilpin, A. *Control of Air Pollution.* London: Butterworths, 1963.

Katz, M. *Measurement of Air Pollutants: Guide to the Selection of Methods.* Geneva: World Health Organisation, 1969.

Lawther, P. J., Martin, A. E. and Wilkins, E. T. *Epidemiology of Air Pollution,* Public Health Papers No. 15. Geneva: World Health Organisation, 1962.

Leighton, P. A. *Photochemistry of Air Pollution.* New York and London: Academic Press, 1961.

Ministry of Health. *Mortality and Morbidity During the London Fog of December, 1952,* Reports on Public Health and Medical Subjects No. 95. London: H.M.S.O., 1954.

Motor Vehicles, Air Pollution, and Health, Report to the U.S. Congress. Washington, D.C.: U.S. Government Printing Office, 1962.

National Academy of Sciences. *Lead: Airborne Lead in Perspective.* Washington, D.C.: 1972.

National Air Pollution Control Administration. *Air Pollution Engineering Manual.* U.S. Public Health Service Publication no. 999—AP—40. Durham, North Carolina: 1967.

Report of the Committee on Air Pollution. Beaver Report Cmnd. 9322. London: H.M.S.O., 1954.

Royal College of Physicians. *Air Pollution and Health.* London: 1970.

Senate Select Committee on Air Pollution. *Air Pollution.* Canberra: Commonwealth Government Printing Office, 1969.

Stern, A. C. ed. *Air Pollution.* 2nd ed., vols. 1, 2 and 3, New York and London: Academic Press, 1968.

U.S. Department of Health, Education and Welfare. *National Air Pollution Control Administration, Publication No.* AP—49, "Air Quality for Particulate Matter", AP—50, "Air Quality Criteria for Sulphur Oxides", AP—51, "Control Techniques for Particulate Air Pollutants", AP—62, "Air Quality Criteria for Carbon Monoxide", AP—63, "Air Quality Criteria for Photochemical Oxidants", AP—64, "Air Quality Criteria for Hydrocarbons", AP—65, "Control Techniques for Carbon Monoxide Emission from Stationary Sources", AP—66, "Control Techniques for Carbon Monoxide, Nitrogen Oxide and Hydrocarbon Emissions from Mobile Sources", AP—67, "Control Techniques for Nitrogen Oxide Emissions from Stationary Sources", AP—68, "Control Techniques for Hydrocarbon and Organic Solvent Emissions from Stationary Sources", Washington, D.C.: U.S. Government Printer.

World Health Organisation. *Air Quality Criteria and Guides for Urban Air Pollutants,* Technical Report Series no. 506. Geneva: 1972.

World Health Organisation. *Air Pollution,* Monograph Series no. 46. Geneva: 1961.

World Health Organisation. *Urban Air Pollution, With Particular Reference to Motor Vehicles,* Technical Report Series no. 410. Geneva, 1969.

WATER POLLUTION CONTROL

Annual Reports. The Water Quality Council of Queensland. Brisbane: Government Printer, 1973 onwards.

Connell, D. W. *Water Pollution: Causes and Effects in Australia.* Brisbane: University of Queensland Press, 1974.

Cowan, E. *Oil and Water: The Torrey Canyon Disaster.* Philadelphia: J. B. Lippincoh, 1968.

Department of the Environment. *Notes on Water Pollution.* London: H.M.S.O., published over several years.

Department of the Environment. *Water Pollution Research.* London: H.M.S.O., published annually.

Department of the Interior. *Water Quality Criteria.* Washington, D.C.: U.S. Government Printing Office, 1968.

Janson, Bengt-Owe, *Ecosystems Approach to the Baltic Problem.* Stockholm: Swedish Natural Science Research Council, 1972.

Kneese, A. V. and Bower, B. T. *Managing Water Quality: Economics, Technology, Institutions.* Baltimore: Johns Hopkins Press, 1968.

Melbourne and Metropolitan Board of Works/Fisheries and Wildlife Division. *Environmental Study of Port Phillip Bay: Report on Phase One 1968–1971.* Melbourne: Ennis and Jarret, 1973.

Ministry of Housing and Local Government. *Final Report of the Trade Effluents Sub-Committee of the Central Advisory Water Committee.* London: H.M.S.O., 1960.

Ministry of Housing and Local Government. *Pollution of the Tidal Thames.* London: H.M.S.O., 1961.

Ministry of Housing and Local Government. *The Purification of the Water of Swimming Baths.* London: H.M.S.O., 1964.

Ministry of Housing and Local Government. *Taken for Granted: Report of the Working Party on Sewage Disposal.* London: H.M.S.O., 1970.

Senate Select Committee on Water Pollution. *Water Pollution in Australia.* Canberra: Commonwealth Government Printing Office, 1970.

Southgate, B. A. *Water: Pollution and Conservation.* Harrow: Thunderbird Enterprises, 1970.

Vollenweider, R. A. *Scientific Fundamentals of the Eutrophication of Lakes and Flowing Waters.* Paris: O.E.C.D., 1970.

Warren, C. E. *Biology and Water Pollution Control,* Philadelphia: W. B. Saunders, 1971.

Warren Spring Laboratory. *Methods of Absorbing Oil Spills at Sea.* London: H.M.S.O., 1968.

Warren Spring Laboratory. *The Torrey Canyon Disaster.* London: H.M.S.O., 1967.

World Health Organisation. *Measurement of the Public Health Importance of Bilharziasis,* Technical Report Series no. 349. Geneva: 1967.

World Health Organisation. *Treatment and Disposal of Wastes,* Technical Report Series no. 367. Geneva: 1967.

World Health Organisation. *Water Pollution Control,* Technical Report Series no. 318. Geneva: 1966.

SOLID WASTE MANAGEMENT

Department of the Environment. *Refuse Disposal: Report of the Working Party on Refuse Disposal.* London: H.M.S.O., 1971.

Ministry of Housing and Local Government. *Disposal of Solid Toxic Wastes: Report of the Technical Committee on the Disposal of Solid Toxic Wastes.* London: H.M.S.O., 1970.

Department of Health, Education and Welfare. *Policies for Solid Waste Management.* Washington, D.C.: U.S. Government Printing Office, 1970.

Environmental Protection Agency. *Composting of Municipal Solid Wastes in the United States,* Washington, D.C.: U.S. Government Printing Office, 1971.

Environmental Protection Agency. *Ocean Disposal of Barge-Delivered Liquid and Solid Wastes from U.S. Coastal Cities.* Washington, D.C.: U.S. Government Printing Office, 1971.

Proceedings of the Australian Waste Disposal Conferences, Sydney: University of New South Wales, 1967, 1971, 1974.

NOISE CONTROL

Bell, A. *Noise.* Geneva: World Health Organisation, 1966.

Lord, P. and Thomas, F. L. *Noise Measurement and Control.* London: Heywood Temple, 1963.

Mills, C. H. G. and Robinson, D. W. *The Subjective Rating of Motor Vehicle Noise,* Cmnd. 2056. London: H.M.S.O., 1963.

National Physical Laboratory. *The Control of Noise,* Symposium no. 12. London: H.M.S.O., 1962.

The Noise Advisory Council. *Aircraft Noise: Flight Routeing Near Airports.* London: H.M.S.O., 1971.

The Noise Advisory Council. *Aircraft Noise: Should the Noise and Number Index be Revised?* London: H.M.S.O., 1972.

The Noise Advisory Council. *Neighbourhood Noise.* London: H.M.S.O., 1971.

The Noise Advisory Council. *Traffic Noise: the Vehicle Regulations and their Enforcement.* London: H.M.S.O., 1972.

Noise Assessment in Residential Areas. Australian Standard 1055—1973. Sydney: Standards Association of Australia, 1973.

Parkin, P. H. and others. *London Noise Survey.* London: H.M.S.O., 1968.

Roskill, The Hon. Mr. Justice. *Commission on the Third London Airport.* London: H.M.S.O., 1969.

Stephenson, R. J. and Vulkan, G. H. *Traffic Noise.* London: Greater London Council, 1968.

Stephenson, R. J. and Vulkan, G. H. *Urban Planning Against Noise.* London: Greater London Council, 1967.

Wilson, Sir A. *Noise: Final Report of the Committee on the Problem of Noise,* Cmnd. 2056. London: H.M.S.O., 1963.

Traffic in Town. The Buchanan Report. London: H.M.S.O., 1963.